Realizing Significance

James Perry

Realizing Significance
Copyright © 2015 by James Perry

All rights reserved. No part of this book may be reproduced or transmitted in any form or by any means without written permission of the author.

Scriptural Citations In Realizing Significance

Unless otherwise noted, the Scriptural Quotations are taken from the New American Standard Bible (1960,1962,1963,1968,1971,1972,1973, 1975,1977,1995) Copyright by The Lockman Foundation. Used within Guideline Permission.

Other Versions Used

The New King James Version (NKJV), © 1982 by Thomas Nelson, Inc. All rights reserved. Used within Guideline Permission.
The Holy Bible, English Standard Version® (ESV®) Copyright © 2001 by Crossway. Used within Guideline Permission.
New International Version (NIV®). Copyright © 1973, 1978, 1984, 2011 by Biblica, Inc.™ All rights reserved worldwide. Used within Guideline Permission.New Living Translation (NLT), Scripture quotations are taken from the *Holy Bible*, New Living Translation, copyright ©1996, 2004, 2007, 2013 by Tyndale House Foundation. Used within Guideline Permission of Tyndale House Publishers, Inc., Carol Stream, Illinois 60188.
The Message (MSG), The Message. Copyright © 1993, 1994, 1995, 1996, 2000, 2001, 2002. Used within Guideline Permission of NavPress Publishing Group.
Other scant references are taken from Williams Translation of the New Testament; J. B. Philipps Translation of the New Testament; and The Amplified Bible. Used within Guideline Permission.

Library of Congress Control Number: 2015930989
ISBN 9780991481194

For a Book Dedication, it is difficult to single out one person over another. There are several people who have had an influence in and on my life. In my formative years, a very ordinary man, one who would himself be thought of as "another little boat", was concerned that the young people in his church would not drift away. To the best of his ability, he tried to do all that he could to keep "the other little boats" within his horizon safe and secure. I will always be grateful to the Lord for Herbie Miller and his friendship.

I also thought about dedicating this book to my seven Great Grandsons and two Great Granddaughters. Their energy and potential is thrilling to observe. These little ones are off to a good start because of the faithful nurturing by their parents. One of them, Keaton Lucas Barron, when he was a two and one half year old, experienced a setback when he was diagnosed with Acute Lymphoblastic Leukemia. By God's grace, there is confidence that this little lamb will survive the intense treatment his small body has received. Two years later, he is progressing well and will complete his weekly treatments at the end of 2015.

Another Great Grandson, Robi, is a rescued little lamb, a Hungarian Gypsy boy who has been adopted into the family of Sam and Mary Beth McLure. They are so committed to Adoption and Foster Care that Sam established his law practice as, "The Adoption Law Firm." Why did he do this and what was his motivation? On his webpage, he has written the following:

"I fell in love with my wife at a Starbucks in Montgomery, Alabama. She was sharing with me her passion for caring for orphans. Her passion resonated with me like a giant gong that shakes your ear drums. After we married we adopted a three year old boy from Hungary.

"I can't really remember what we were thinking back then that led us to choose adoption as the means for caring for the fatherless...our once fatherless son. I mean, what James says is to "visit" the orphans in their affliction. What does that mean? Does that mean that Christians have to adopt orphans to be obedient? I don't think so.

"There are other ways of caring for the fatherless besides adoption. We could have started volunteering at a local orphanage or partnered with DHR in foster care. We could have given money to an adoption fund to help relieve the financial burden of someone else adopting. We could have planned a mission trip to a far away orphanage in Romania or India. We could have tried to start an orphanage ourselves. All of those things would have been good; and we may still do them...all of them. But, of all the strategies for caring for the fatherless, I can't shake the feeling that there's something special about adoption. Take our son for example. When we legally finalized his adoption, in a small town near Budapest, we had to choose a name for him. We chose to name him after me, and call him the second; Samuel Jacob McLure, II. I named him that. I gave him my name, because he is mine. He is my son, and I love him dearly. We didn't adopt him because he is beautiful (though he is that). We didn't adopt him because he is smart (though he is that). We didn't adopt him because we knew he would always be obedient (because he isn't). We didn't adopt him because he has perfect health (because he doesn't). We adopted him because we love him. I named him Samuel Jacob McLure II, because I never want him to doubt that he is mine...I have called him by name." You can read more by going to:

The Adoption Law Firm
www.TheAdoptionFirm.com
You can call or write:
Mailing Address: P.O. Box 2396
Montgomery, AL 36102
Phone: 334-612-3406

I am honored to have family members with this level of commitment and practice of pure religion. It is a joy and privilege to Dedicate this Book to: Samuel Jacob McLure, Attorney At Law.

He, along with my Granddaughter Mary Beth Perry McLure have two sons, Robi (Samuel Jacob McLure, II, now 7 years old)) and Andrew Glen McLure. They were recently blest with a daughter, Mary Claire McLure born in October 2014. In their lives, Sam and Mary Beth have faithfully implemented James 1:27 (NLT), "Pure and lasting religion in the sight of God our Father means that we must care for orphans and widows in their troubles, and refuse to let the world corrupt us."

With the little lambs entrusted to them by the Lord, they have also implemented and are practicing the words of wisdom in Proverbs 22:6 (NLT), "Teach your children to choose the right path, and when they are older, they will remain upon it." This young family is both a challenge and a blessing for and in my life. I feel blest beyond measure. May such labor for the Lord be blest and a blessing to many others.

Preface

There are times when one can be overwhelmed by the turmoil of life and the sense of helplessness to alleviate a particular situation. When one's ability is expended to a point of near-exhaustion, one becomes desperate for relief and would welcome it from someone – anyone who can make a difference and turn one's tempest into tranquility. This was the case after the Disciples took Jesus onto their vessel and set sail. All started out well until the unexpected occurred, namely, a fierce windstorm at sea. The incident is recorded in Mark 4:36-37 (NKJV), "Now when they had left the multitude, they took Him along in the boat as He was. And other little boats were also with Him. And a great windstorm arose, and the waves beat into the boat, so that it was already filling." Something is unique about Mark's account of this event. He inserts a phrase, "…other little boats were also with Him…" In the ebb and flow of one's life, there are almost always the "other little boats" that are part of one's landscape and horizon. One may not always notice or be aware of them, but they are there just the same.

One can muse regarding why Mark included this phrase. Could it be part of his own life experience? Might it be a reflection of a moment of failure in his own life, the time when he was not as faithful to the task at hand, not viewed as being a dependable servant in the ministry? There is a hint of an incident that occurred while ministry was being done and Mark failed to participate. One gets a glimpse of the depth of feeling about this incident in Acts 15:36-40, "Then after some days Paul said to Barnabas, Let us now go back and visit our brethren in every city where we have preached the word of the Lord, and see how they are doing. Now Barnabas was determined to take with them John called Mark. But Paul insisted that they should not take with them the one who had departed from them in Pamphylia, and had not gone with them to the work. Then the contention became so sharp that they parted from one another. And so Barnabas took Mark and sailed to Cyprus; but Paul chose Silas and departed, being commended by the brethren to the grace of God."

It would be a reoccurring thought for John Mark as he began to realize the depth and scope of his failure and his being unwanted, set aside from future ministry with the Apostle Paul. He had become like one of the "other little boats" that were caught in the storm except that his cousin Barnabas, ever the encourager, refused to let John Mark sink or drift aimlessly away. For the next few years, John Mark would travel with Barnabas. One can imagine the internal gnawing within John Mark about his failure and lack of dependability. One wonders what his prayer might have been and the confession of his soul before the Lord! Perhaps it was similar to the words of the second stanza penned by Mary A. Baker in the Hymn "Master, The Tempest Is Raging", written in 1874 - - -

Master, with anguish of spirit, I bow in my grief today;
The depths of my sad heart are troubled. Oh, waken and save,
I pray!
Torrents of sin and of anguish, Sweep o'er my sinking soul;
And I perish! I perish! dear Master, Oh, hasten, and take control.

Barnabas and Mark pressed on in their ministry effort and then, maybe ten or twelve years later, a note arrived from the Apostle Paul. In II Timothy 4:11 (NKJV), Paul wrote, "...Get Mark and bring him with you, for he is useful to me for ministry." The Message Paraphrase renders this text, "Bring Mark with you; he'll be my right-hand man." Can this really be true? Does Paul want Mark to return and to be part of the ministry with him once again? Can a failure be found trustworthy to be Paul's "right-hand man"? Can a "little boat" be seaworthy once again? The answer is, "Yes!"

There are many lessons one can glean from the life of John Mark in his experience and ministry. Not the least of these is that a momentary failure does not need to be viewed as final. The "little boat" does not have to drift or sink. It can be repaired and become functional once again. The incident with Paul and Mark also serves as an opportunity for one to remember to leave room for repentance and restoration. There should be a time to forgive, forget and to re-establish one in all areas – especially in kingdom ministry.

As this book progresses, the "other little boats" will serve as a metaphor for the many who for one reason or another are construed to be the "little people" and the "other sheep" one encounters along the way. The hope is that you will be one who does not ignore or overlook those who are deemed by some to be unimportant, inconsequential, unworthy or insignificant. One should be willing to be like Barnabas who came alongside of Mark, nurturing and encouraging him to the point where he would be seen as useful rather than useless and profitable rather than unprofitable.

May the following pages assist you to gain a vision for ministry and development of a strategy and an effort that will impact your culture. The vision statement of three Institutions (Columbia Bible College in Columbia, SC now Columbia International University; Covenant College, Lookout Mountain, GA; and Covenant Theological Seminary in St. Louis, MO) where this writer attended could serve as a starting point for your worldview and vision statement: "To Know Him and To Make Him Known" and "In All Things, Christ Preeminent." The theme hymn was the same for both of these schools of learning. The words were sung to different tunes but the thrust and commitment called for remained the same.

All for Jesus, all for Jesus! All my being's ransomed powers:

All my thoughts and words and doings, All my days and all my hours.

Let my hands perform His bidding, Let my feet run in His ways;
Let my eyes see Jesus only, Let my lips speak forth His praise.

Since my eyes were fixed on Jesus, I've lost sight of all beside;
So enchained my spirit's vision, Looking at the Crucified.

> Words By: Mary D. James (1871)

At the end of the day, may you be one who can and will say, "But by the grace of God I am what I am, and His grace toward me was not in vain; but I labored more abundantly than they all, yet not I, but the grace of God which was with me" (I Corinthians 15:10). Sola De Gloria.

Table of Contents

1. A Serious Evaluation 1
2. A Serious Follow Through 9
3. A Serious Understanding 19
4. A Serious Reminder 29
5. A Serious Test 39
6. A Serious Strategy 51
7. A Serious Challenge 65
8. A Serious Trend 79
9. A Serious Drift 97
10. A Serious Defining Moment 111
11. A Serious Possibility 125
12. A Serious Acknowledgement 143
13. A Serious Performance 161

Concluding Thoughts 171

1. A Serious Evaluation

There are different ways of looking at one's world: (a) there is a rapid deterioration and departure from foundational principles and moral values that will lead to its demise and destruction, or (b) there are vast opportunities where one can make a difference in the life or lives of others, or (c) by impacting the culture positively to the degree that one can. It will include an approach where one will be aware of the "other little boats" and the many so-called and designated "little people" and "other sheep" who are here and a part of our lives regardless of whether or not we welcome or ignore them.

In a recent personal Blog, the biblical idea regarding the "little boats, little people and other sheep" was framed with this question: "What kind of sense and commitment does the Christian and Church have in terms of personal involvement with orphans? Is the involvement anywhere close to James 1:22-27 (NIV), "Do not merely listen to the word, and so deceive yourselves. Do what it says...Religion that God our Father accepts as pure and faultless is this: to look after orphans and widows in their distress and to keep oneself from being polluted by the world..." James 2:16-17 (NIV) asks and declares: "If one of you says to him, Go, I wish you well; keep warm and well fed, but does nothing about his physical needs, what good is it? In the same way, faith by itself, if it is not accompanied by action, is dead..." The *Message Paraphrase* of verse 17 is direct: "Isn't it obvious that God-talk without God-acts is outrageous nonsense?"

There are two recent events and experiences that indicate the urgency of this practical instruction being applied in one's worldview and practice. The first is from the devotional, *Today In The Word*, on July 5, 2012 by Dave Branon entitled, "My Buddy

William." He writes: "As we got off the bus at a home for mentally and physically challenged children in Copse, Jamaica, I didn't expect to find a football player. While the teen choir and the other adult chaperones dispersed to find kids to hug, love, and play with, I came upon a young man named William. I'm not sure what William's medical diagnosis was, but he looked like he probably had cerebral palsy. I had grabbed a football before getting off the bus, so I tossed it gently to William, who dropped it. But when I picked it up and put it into his hands, he slowly manipulated it until he had it just how he wanted it. Then, leaning back against a railing for balance, William tossed a perfect spiral. For the next 45 minutes, we played toss and catch—he tossed, I caught. William laughed and laughed—and stole my heart. On that day he had as much impact on me, I'm sure, as I did on him. He taught me that we are all needed as a part of Christ's body, the church (1 Corinthians 12:20-25)."

He went on to comment: "People often dismiss others who are different from themselves. But it is the Williams of the world who teach us that joy can come when we accept others and respond in compassion. Is there a William in your world who needs you to be his buddy?" He closes his devotional with a prayer, "Lord, help us to see how much we need each other in our Christian walk. May we show Your love to others who are different than us. Give us an open heart to learn. Amen." He adds: "We need one another in order to be who God wants us to be." William is just one of the many "little boats" and "little people" and "other sheep" who are too often ignored by others.

The second event and experience was the result of a note on Facebook as a Mother wrote about her adopted son and his fifth Birthday in July 2013. In a very moving and touching way, she wrote: "Five years ago a little gypsy boy was born in a rural Hungarian hospital. He was three weeks early, blind in one eye, had a scary-sounding infection, and his mother left him. I didn't know anything about it, but that little boy was my son. We missed the first 3 years, 4 months, and 2 days of his life and I will always be sad for that loss. But today we get to celebrate our sweet, crazy, funny, Hungarian Gypsy Alabama Batman boy. And it's gonna be exciting!" He is a friendly and active little boy who has responded well to the care and affection from those who have become part of his life. He is another of the "little boats" and "little people" and "other sheep/lambs" who are so easily overlooked.

When one thinks about the multitude of orphans throughout the world, representing many different language and ethnic groups, a consideration surfaces in terms of how one can communicate with an orphan who does not know the language of a host country, and in all likelihood has not come from a familial setting where biblical love was part of a daily experience and interaction. Even though some might say that the universal language of love should be able to communicate adequately, what if the person has never been in a place or context where love was displayed and experienced? What if the person had no living and working definition of what love actually is? A person who has been an orphan all of her or his life, what familial sense of love can one expect her or him to have learned and know? In looking into the eyes of an immigrant or an orphan, many times there is that blank stare and a helplessness that is obvious. The person seems to project they are lost and needing assistance. They may be guarding against the unexpected and unwanted, responding from a desire to protect oneself from the unknown. One can only empathize with the lonely, empty and frustrating feelings that this person is experiencing.

This type of a situation and experience is reminiscent of my years as a teenager and being included as part of a gospel team that went to various places. One such place was Ellis Island in New York Harbor that served as the entry point for Immigrants coming into this country for the first time. The setting was not all that lovely. Basically, it was a large terminal-type facility with little by way of accommodations. I still remember seeing a woman sitting on her suitcase in that terminal all alone and unable to communicate. Her look was one of confusion and fear. I often wonder what she was thinking and how she was feeling? I wonder if she had a family member already in this country who had promised to be there for her but hadn't yet arrived? I wonder if anyone ever did arrive for her or would she continue alone, afraid and unable to communicate. I was so young and wish now it was possible to have a "do-over" chance to make that soul feel wanted and needed. However, we would go and play our instruments, give a testimony and someone would give a message, talk or brief sermon. The problem with the message, talk or brief sermon was not the content but the inability of most of those sitting in the terminal to understand what was being communicated. The only indication of understanding was when we would play the old hymns of the Church. At that moment, the universal language of music was able to convey a message. Perhaps that moment of hearing the music to a hymn gave the stranger, one of the "huddled masses yearning to be free," a remembrance of the Love of God in Christ. This is just an early experience with some of the "other little boats, little people and the other sheep."

    One additional thought that needs to be present in one's thinking pertains to love and how "I" understand it and how "My" body language exhibits it. How real is biblical love in "My" life? How readily do "I" exhibit I Corinthians 13:4-8 in "My" life as it is lived in this culture and at this time? In *The Message Paraphrase*, the passage states: "...no matter what I say, what I believe, and what I do, I'm bankrupt without love. Love never gives up. Love cares more for others than for self. Love doesn't want what it doesn't have. Love doesn't strut, Doesn't have a swelled head, Doesn't force itself on others, Isn't always me first, Doesn't fly off the handle, Doesn't keep score of the sins of others, Doesn't revel when others grovel, Takes pleasure in the flowering of truth, Puts up with anything, Trusts God always, Always looks for the best, Never looks back, But keeps going to the end. Love never dies..." Does this represent your love; my love; our love in this world and culture? Will others be attracted to Jesus Christ because of what they are able to observe in us, the reality of biblically defined love being lived out before the watching world?

In thinking about the orphans and the unwanted, the homeless and the needy multitudes in our world, two different thoughts occur. The first thought pertains to the words of The New Colossus etched on the base of The Statue of Liberty, "Give me your tired, your poor, your huddled masses yearning to breathe free, the wretched refuse of your teeming shore. Send these, the homeless, tempest-tossed to me, I lift my lamp beside the golden door." One may have some difficulty grappling with the phrase, "the wretched refuse of your teeming shore." Can this be how the stranger entering this nation feels when all alone and being thrust into a group of people who are unknown? The second thought that occurred and that may give some encouragement is in the Lyric written by Bill and Gloria Gaither and sung so meaningfully by Sandi Patti. It is entitled: "Love In Any Language." As the lyric spans the globe, one reoccurring expression is: "Love in any language, Straight from the heart, Pulls us all together, Never apart." The next lines capture the expression of I Corinthians 13, "And once we learn to speak it, All the world will hear, Love in any language, Fluently spoken here."

We should be grateful and supportive of the organizations and individuals who genuinely care about and for the widow, the orphan, the stranger, the homeless, the unwanted and "the wretched refuse of your teeming shore". Even though there are some who will take advantage of one's benevolence or maybe even abuse it, there will be those who will appreciate the kindness and generosity. They will more than make up for the "user-types" who seek only that which will give them some material benefit. One should be motivated to serving others by the words in I Timothy 6:17-18 (NKJV), "Command those who are rich in this present age not to be haughty, nor to trust in uncertain riches but in the living God, who gives us richly all things to enjoy. Let them do good, that they be rich in good works, ready to give, willing to share…"

APPLICATIONS and QUESTIONS:

Presently, how well do you implement James 1:22-27, "Do not merely listen to the word, and so deceive yourselves," or do you "Do what it says…?"

Does your practice of religion look similar to "Religion that God our Father accepts as pure and faultless which is this: to look after orphans and widows in their distress…?" Do you view others as being insignificant or unworthy of one's attention and care?

Is this passage intended for you today or was it merely a passing thought for those in the first century?

What about the implication of James 2:16-17, "If one of you says to him (the one hungry, naked, homeless), Go, I wish you well; keep warm and well fed, but does nothing about his physical needs, what good is it? In the same way, faith by itself, if it is not accompanied by action, is dead."

Does The Message paraphrase clarify verse 17 for you: "Isn't it obvious that God-talk without God-acts is outrageous nonsense…?"

What is your commitment? What will it be as you purpose to put into practice the words of Scripture listed above?

It is not enough to be busy; so are the ants.
The question is: what are we busy about?
— Henry David Thoreau

If you have a purpose in which you can believe,
there's no end to the amount of things you can accomplish.
— Marian Anderson

2. A Serious Follow Through

It is one thing to be able to evaluate the times in which one lives and to sense the gravity of the many needs that seemingly abound everywhere, but it is another thing altogether to follow through and to do as much as one can for as many as one can. The previous chapter concluded by asking: How do you implement James 1:22-27 (NIV)? James wrote, "Do not merely listen to the word, and so deceive yourselves. Do what it says…Religion that God our Father accepts as pure and faultless is this: to look after orphans and widows in their distress…" Is this passage intended for you today or was it merely a passing thought for those in the first century?

A place for focus would be in the area of the neglected children in the world. These are the children who through no fault of their own are either unwanted by a birth parent, are made available for adoption or are abandoned for placement in a foster care system. In 2010, Focus on the Family published an article by Katie Overstreet entitled, "Adoption From Foster Care." Her article begins with, "Although many children in foster care have special needs, they are in need of a family as much as any waiting child." She also states this very significant statement by an adopted child, "There is never so much love in the world that reaching out is a bad idea."

In Matthew 19:13-15 (NIV), there is a glimpse of an interesting and important aspect of Jesus' ministry seen in His focus upon children. The text states, "Then little children were brought to Jesus for him to place his hands on them and pray for them. But the disciples rebuked those who brought them. Jesus said, let the little children come to me, and do not hinder them, for the kingdom of heaven belongs to such as these. When he had placed his hands on them, he went on from there." The key is His concern and focus on, "Let the little children come to Me…" It is reminiscent of a Sunday School song that was sung years ago: "Jesus Loves the little children, All the children of the world. Red and yellow, black/brown white, all are precious in His sight, Jesus Loves the little children of the world." The song had merit then, as well as now.

    The neglect and needs of children around the world seems to steadily increase. In 2005 and 2006, the following report was given in London, UK: "Hundreds of millions of children are suffering from severe exploitation and discrimination and have become virtually invisible to the world, UNICEF (United Nations International Children's Emergency Fund) said today in a major report that explores the causes of exclusion and the abuses children experience…millions of children disappear from view when trafficked or forced to work in domestic servitude. Other children, such as street children, live in plain sight but are excluded from fundamental services and protections. Not only do these children endure abuse, most are shut out from school, healthcare and other vital services they need to grow and thrive. 'The State of the World's Children 2006: Excluded and Invisible' is a sweeping assessment of the world's most vulnerable children, whose rights to a safe and healthy childhood are exceptionally difficult to protect. These children are growing up beyond the reach of development campaigns and are often invisible in everything from public debate and legislation, to statistics and news stories. Without focused attention, millions of children will remain trapped and forgotten in childhood and suffer neglect and abuse, with devastating consequences for their long-term well-being and the development of entire nations. The report argues that any society with an interest in the welfare of its children and its own future must not allow this to happen." If that is even remotely close to being the state and condition of children in the world, how much more meaningful are the words of Jesus, "Let the little children come to Me…" It is equally vital that the biblical follower of Jesus Christ share His focus regarding the little ones, the lambs who are to be cared for and nurtured.

On another occasion, Jesus had made a significant point in Matthew 18:1-6 (NIV), "At that time the disciples came to Jesus and asked: Who is the greatest in the kingdom of heaven? He called a little child and had him stand among them. And he said: I tell you the truth, unless you change and become like little children, you will never enter the kingdom of heaven. Therefore, whoever humbles himself like this child is the greatest in the kingdom of heaven. And whoever welcomes a little child like this in my name welcomes me. But if anyone causes one of these little ones who believe in me to sin, it would be better for him to have a large millstone hung around his neck and to be drowned in the depths of the sea." The Disciples sounded as if they were concerned with a "pecking order" and some kind of "rank" in terms of God's Kingdom. The question is revealing, "Who is the greatest in the Kingdom of Heaven?" they asked. Jesus was on His way to the cross of guilt and shame, whereas the disciples were concerned with a position of prestige and honor. The answer given by Jesus is not what they were desiring to hear: "Unless you change and become like little children, you will never enter the kingdom of heaven. Therefore, whoever humbles himself like this child is the greatest in the kingdom of heaven." To become like little children and to humble oneself like this child, that's the path to greatness in the Kingdom. Are the disciples ready to give their response? What should the response be? As they listen and ponder the words of Jesus, the obvious answer coming from Jesus Christ and the manner in which He expects His disciples to respond leaves the only valid and logical answer possible which is "Yes!"

The Focus on the Family article from 2010 indicates: "Currently, nearly 500,000 children and youth are in the United States foster care system. These children have all entered the system due to abuse, neglect or abandonment on the part of the birth parent. Of those children in foster care, between 120,000 and 130,000 are considered legal orphans and are awaiting adoption into a permanent family. For these children, a birth parent's rights had to be terminated because they were unable to provide a safe and secure home for the kids. Now they are waiting for someone to give them a second chance." Children Uniting Nations (2007) reports that 463,000 children enter foster care for several reasons: "18.8% Physical Abuse; 7.9% Emotional abuse; 6.2% Sexual Abuse; 3.2% Caretaker Inability (Source: Los Angeles Department of Children and Family Services, 2007)." The study also indicates, "What happens to foster youth who emancipate (age-out) from the system?" The data indicates: "65% emancipate without a place to live; Less than 3% go to college; 51% are unemployed; Emancipated females are 4 times more likely to receive public assistance than the general population; In any given year, foster children compromise less than 0.3% of the state's population, and yet 40% of persons living in homeless shelters are former foster children. A similarly disproportionate percentage of the nation's prison population is comprised of former foster youth." These "little lambs" were allowed to exist without adequate care, guidance or instruction. They never should've been viewed as inconsequential, unwanted or expendable. It is sad that no one interceded in their behalf with care, compassion and seeking to make a positive difference during their formative years.

In the midst of his personal suffering, there is a very compelling part of Job's Discourse recorded in Job 29:11-16 (NIV), "Whoever heard me spoke well of me, and those who saw me commended me, because I rescued the poor who cried for help, and the fatherless who had none to assist him. The man who was dying blessed me; I made the widow's heart sing. I put on righteousness as my clothing; justice was my robe and my turban. I was eyes to the blind and feet to the lame. I was a father to the needy; I took up the case of the stranger." How many would be able to echo the words of Job, "I was a father to the needy; I took up the case of the stranger?" This is an example of the minimal concern every child of God should know and be guided by, to be concerned for those in need and motivated to act and alleviate as much hardship as possible. Does this serve as a reminder and challenge for you to do something more than pray for the oppressed and needy? Do you realize it is more than sending a contribution to some organization to act in your behalf? Do you sense and see why and how you can be engaged in making a difference in the lives of the needy, neglected, insignificant or unwanted?

When the people of God become engaged in the great task of care for the little children of the world, lambs that Jesus wants His followers to care for and nurture, it will become part of the fiber, the spiritual DNA representing who we are in terms of Kingdom ministry. An illustration of how this can become a real part of one's life is shared in the following account. A prospective adoptive parent recently wrote in a prayer letter, "I was teaching kids Sunday School and the lesson had to do with the benefits of being adopted by God. The kids weren't listening very well, and I was not teaching very well, and I finally I just told them why I couldn't concentrate. All of the sudden, the importance of adoption hit me and I broke down and cried in front of the kids. That's not the lesson they were expecting to hear today, I imagine (although they DID start paying attention)." There's something very meaningful in those words, "The benefits of being adopted by God."

It is of benefit to consider spiritual adoption. One should have a clear understanding of what it is, and how it occurs. The *Westminster Shorter Catechism* asks and answers (#33), "What is Adoption?" The answer given is, "Adoption is an act of God's free grace, whereby we are received into the number, and have the right to all the privileges of the sons of God." At least three areas are noted: Adoption is an act of God's free grace; Adoption allows one to be received into the number of all other elect ones; and adoption extends to the elect one all the privileges of the sons of God." One passage of God's Word that is helpful in understanding adoption and election is Galatians 4:4-7 (NIV). The text states: "What I am saying is that as long as the heir is a child, he is no different from a slave, although he owns the whole estate. He is subject to guardians and trustees until the time set by his father. So also, when we were children, we were in slavery under the basic principles of the world. But when the time had fully come, God sent his Son, born of a woman, born under law, to redeem those under law, that we might receive the full rights of sons. Because you are sons, God sent the Spirit of his Son into our hearts, the Spirit who calls out, Abba, Father. So you are no longer a slave, but a son; and since you are a son, God has made you also an heir." The *New Living Translation* renders verses 4-7, "But when the right time came, God sent his Son, born of a woman, subject to the law. God sent him to buy freedom for us who were slaves to the law, so that he could adopt us as his very own children. And because you Gentiles have become his children, God has sent the Spirit of his Son into your hearts, and now you can call God your dear Father. Now you are no longer a slave but God's own child. And since you are his child, everything he has belongs to you." Another biblical reference that echoes these same thoughts is John 1:10-13 (NIV), "He (Jesus) was in the world, and though the world was made through him, the world did not recognize him. He came to that which was his own, but his own did not receive him. Yet to all who received him, to those who believed in his name, he gave the right to become children of God, children born not of natural descent, nor of human decision or a husband's will, but born of God." Jesus "gave us the right to become children of God…" It was not based upon natural descent, or human decision, or a husband's will but born of God. This is what it means to be adopted by God as one becomes a member His family.

In the physical sense and for the parentless child, the orphan or foster care child, a new relationship comes into being. The child is able to address one intimately as "Abba, Father" (spiritually) or "Daddy" (physically). It is based on a decision and choice by one who was motivated by compassion and familial love to enlarge a family to include one who did not know a family and the stability of a functional home. There is a touching account shared by one who was a well-known minister. He told of an incident pertaining to his adopted child. The child reached a place of wanting to call the adoptive father by his first name. After a while, he visited with his child and shared words along this line, "There are many, many people in this country and world who call me Jim, but you are the only one who has the legal right and privilege to call me Daddy or Father." He went on to say that from that point forward the matter had been settled. It was now "Dad" and "Father" for his child. It underscores the special bond and relationship that comes into being when one is adopted into a family.

The Focus on the Family article also states, "The reality is that kids in foster care move from home to home for any or no reason at all. Many feel unwanted and unloved as they have no permanency in their lives. The fact that they have their basic needs met, a roof over their heads and food to eat, pales in comparison to the need for a permanent and consistent family. Many children in foster care may have one or more special needs. These needs include siblings also in need of a family, prenatal exposure to drugs or alcohol, developmental delays and those who are older than five or are minorities. The sooner they find permanency, the better. For the majority of these kids, they have been given a label or a stigma that tends to identify them as 'not good enough' or 'second class.' But we know the reality that these kids are as loved by God as any child." These children deserve the chance to be part of a family where they can experience the reality of family, the stability of a functional home and the intimacy of love in a familial way. There are fine Christian orphanages in this nation and many throughout the world. They try to establish and maintain a home and family atmosphere for the orphan or unwanted child. However, it is not the same as one who knows they are wanted as a part of a real and viable family where they will be accepted and cared for or where they will know and gain the sense that they belong. That is true physically and it is true spiritually as well.

More than forty years ago, Bill and Gloria Gaither wrote the words to: "The Family of God." A stanza and chorus is apropos in this focus on the unwanted child and orphan:

> From the door of an orphanage to the house of the King,
> No longer an outcast, a new song I sing;
> From rags unto riches, from the weak to the strong,
> I'm not worthy to be here, but praise God I belong!
> I'm so glad I'm a part of the family of God...

APPLICATIONS and QUESTIONS:

What is your level of feeling and compassion toward those who are orphans, foster children, and needy?

Do you think Jesus wants you to think as He thought when He said, "Allow the children to come to Me?" Do you have time for the children?

In your own biblical knowledge, what do you see as a benefit of you being adopted into the family of God and the Kingdom of heaven?

Because of that adoption, is there any obligation on your part to those who have not yet been brought into the family? Are you able to do this without any restriction or reluctance?

Do you think the key for you is (a) to make a contribution to some organization, or (b) to invest your life into the life of another? Why did you answer the way you did?

Read Matthew 7:20-23 and see how Jesus would assess what you do and how you do it? Is it according to His will or good deeds that you hope will cause your answer to be acceptable?

What would be His determination regarding you and your deeds and efforts? Would your deeds and efforts be acceptable to Him? What do you think He would say about your deeds and efforts?

My adoption was treated as a celebration.
Shouldn't every one of our children be able to say the same?
Michael Reagan

3. A Serious Understanding

As we have noted, the culture can exert its influence in many ways, not the least of which is the way it views its children. For a long time, there has been the evolving notion: "children should be seen but not heard." It has now degenerated to the point where there is considerable child abuse and cruelty of all sorts and degrees. With greater awareness, one would think abuse would be decreasing, but sadly, it continues at an alarming and increasing rate. The "little boats, little people, and other sheep" are many times being ignored or deemed as unimportant even when they are being mistreated and maltreated. Why should we focus on those who are being mistreated? Simply because of what it means and involves for one to suffer at the hands of another, i.e. "to treat badly, cruelly, or inconsiderately." This needs to be weighed against the biblical view of who and what children are considered to be, "Behold, children are a heritage from the Lord, the fruit of the womb a reward. Like arrows in the hand of a warrior are the children of one's youth. Blessed is the man who fills his quiver with them" (Psalm 127:3-5, ESV)! The children, some of whom are the "little boats, little people, or other sheep," should never be viewed as a nuisance, inconsequential or insignificant but as living souls entrusted to the care of a loving parent who will nurture that child and enable him or her to be all of what the Lord wants that little one to be and become.

However, there is also a dark and stark reality in our world. The Yahoo Contributor Network (October 28, 2010) published the following General Statistics. "Many children suffer from neglect or abuse that is hidden. The reports of child abuse of some nature are three million a year in the United States. There are about five children that die each day from physical child abuse. Of these five killed, three are under the age of four. Concerning sexual abuse, 90 percent know the criminal. In fact, 68 percent are a member of the family. Child abuse or neglect of some nature can occur in any religion; also in all levels of education, cultures even social or economic levels. The statistics say that of all the women in prison in the United States, 31 percent were abused as a child. With the people that are in rehabilitation centers, 60 percent reported child abuse or neglect as a child. From the children that are abused or neglected 30 percent will become an abuser. Eighty percent of abused children at age of 21 or over will have some form of psychological disorder. In the prisons for men 14 percent were abused when children."

An organization calling itself Dream Catchers For Abused Children has published their list of statistics (September 2014): "48% of abused children are boys; 52% of abused children are girls; 45% of abused children are white race; 22% of abused children are African American race; 22% of abused children are Hispanic race." They also include a section to show the "Dramatic Increase In Child Abuse Statistics - Abuse and Neglect of American Children Has Increased 134% since 1980; Physical Abuse Has Increased 84% since 1980; Sexual Abuse Has Increased 350% since 1980; Emotional Abuse Has Increased 333% since 1980; Child Neglect Abuse Has Increased 320% since 1980…" On their Facebook page, they have their Mission Statement Published. It states the following: "To educate the public on all aspects of Child Abuse such as symptoms, intervention, prevention, statistics, reporting, and helping victims locate the proper resources necessary to achieve a full recovery. We also cover areas such as bullying, teen suicide and prevention, children's rights, child trafficking, missing and exploited children, online safety, and pedophiles/child molesters." Just a thought and a question: Should the Christian and the Church be engaged in this type of awareness and effort regarding the "little boats, little people, and other sheep" within its sphere of ministry?

There also needs to be a diligent effort to counteract child pornography and pedophilia that is occurring not only in the culture at large, but also within organized religion. It is appalling how the cultural behavior has penetrated and infiltrated the culture organized religion.

Another area not often referred to as abuse is abortion. It is incredible to even think that there is a readiness and willingness to abort unwanted babies prevailing in our country and world. Christian Life Resources reports on the United States Abortion Statistics from 1973 to 2012. The total number of abortions in that time-frame was at 54,559,615. Their information was based upon data coming from "Two independent sources, (a) the government's Centers for Disease Control (CDC) and (b) the Guttmacher Institute (GI), which was once a special research affiliate of abortion chain Planned Parenthood." One can only wonder about what this nation has allowed for the past 40 plus years. How many scholars, medical professionals, scientists, civic and national leaders have wound up in a bucket at the foot of an abortion table, put to death by a human act of the will. These were souls who never had the opportunity of joining with the Psalmist and saying, "I praise you, for I am fearfully and wonderfully made. Wonderful are your works; my soul knows it very well. My frame was not hidden from you, when I was being made in secret, intricately woven in the depths of the earth. Your eyes saw my unformed substance; in your book were written, every one of them, the days that were formed for me, when as yet there was none of them…" (Psalm 139:14-16 - NIV). *The Message Paraphrase* expresses these verses. " I thank you, High God - you're breathtaking! Body and soul, I am marvelously made! I worship in adoration - what a creation! You know me inside and out, you know every bone in my body; You know exactly how I was made, bit by bit, how I was sculpted from nothing into something. Like an open book, you watched me grow from conception to birth; all the stages of my life were spread out before you, The days of my life all prepared before I'd even lived one day."

One can only wonder how the heart of God must grieve and ache over the slaughter of these innocent ones. One can also wonder about the silence of so many in light of so many being aborted and put to a premature death. What happened to the concern referenced in Proverbs 31:8-9 (NIV), "Speak up for those who cannot speak for themselves, for the rights of all who are destitute. Speak up and judge fairly; defend the rights of the poor and needy"? Or, where are those who as The New Living Translation expresses it, "Speak up for those who cannot speak for themselves; ensure justice for those who are perishing. Yes, speak up for the poor and helpless, and see that they get justice…" Are these just "little boats, little people and other sheep" who do not matter? Isn't this an atrocity that should be addressed? Should one remain silent when an atrocity is occurring? Even if it is risky, aren't we supposed to run that risk and speak up for those who cannot speak for themselves? These questions are not merely rhetorical? As biblical Christians, we are not afforded the luxury of being indifferent to the "little boats, little people and the other sheep/lambs" on our radar screen!

The Gospel of Matthew records a horrendous activity that took place at the time of the birth of Jesus Christ. In Matthew 2:16-18 (ESV), there is recorded the extent of Infanticide taking place in an effort to kill the Lord Jesus Christ. The text records, "Then Herod, when he saw that he had been tricked by the wise men, became furious, and he sent and killed all the male children in Bethlehem and in all that region who were two years old or under, according to the time that he had ascertained from the wise men. Then was fulfilled what was spoken by the prophet Jeremiah: A voice was heard…weeping and loud lamentation, Rachel weeping for her children; she refused to be comforted, because they are no more." Mary and Joseph escaped with the baby Jesus into Egypt, where they would remain, until after the death of King Herod. It's understandable how and why Jesus would have an affinity toward the little ones and the children. He would incorporate the children into different teaching sessions as He made application of a behavior that had to be learned and a model that needed to be followed.

There is an irony with the escape into Egypt to spare the life of the infant Jesus. One should remember the scene in Egypt 1500 BC. It is recorded in Exodus 1:15-22 (NIV). "Then the king of Egypt spoke to the Hebrew midwives and he said: When you do the duties of a midwife for the Hebrew women, and see them on the birth-stools, if it is a son, then you shall kill him; but if it is a daughter, then she shall live. But the midwives feared God, and did not do as the king of Egypt commanded them, but saved the male children alive. So the king of Egypt called for the midwives and said to them, Why have you done this thing, and saved the male children alive? And the midwives said to Pharaoh, Because the Hebrew women are not like the Egyptian women; for they are lively and give birth before the midwives come to them. Therefore God dealt well with the midwives, and the people multiplied and grew very mighty…So Pharaoh commanded all his people…Every son who is born you shall cast into the river, and every daughter you shall save alive." The king was fearful of the growth of the Hebrew population and what it might mean in the future if the male children were allowed to live. To protect and preserve his own vested interest, and that of the nation, he ordered that the male children should be drowned. Exodus 2:1-4 (NKJV) records how the parents of Moses ran a risk in an attempt to save their son's life. The text states, "And a man of the house of Levi went and took as wife a daughter of Levi. So the woman conceived and bore a son. And when she saw that he was a beautiful child, she hid him three months. But when she could no longer hide him, she took an ark of bulrushes for him, daubed it with asphalt and pitch, put the child in it, and laid it in the reeds by the river's bank. And his sister (Miriam) stood afar off, to know what would be done to him."

Today in the Word for December 5, 2014 included: "Every year, nearly three million babies worldwide die in their first month. Sometimes the problem is just staying warm enough, especially for premature or underweight infants. To help address this, Jane Chen co-founded Embrace, an organization that works to save these vulnerable children. They have developed a special infant warmer for use by mothers in undeveloped or resource-limited countries." The devotional inserts this account in a context of an infant being placed in a small ark and left at the water's edge in proximity to the place where the Egyptian Princess often came. The devotional asks some obvious and practical questions regarding why she rescued the baby: "Did the princess's motherly instincts kick in? Did she sympathize with the plight of the slaves? Or was it general human compassion for a helpless child? We don't know exactly, but whatever the reason, she acted to preserve life. The political implications of her decision would have been immense. She lived in the house of Pharaoh, who had ordered all the newborn baby boys of the Hebrew slaves to be killed. It was a murderous tactic to control their population (Exodus 1:22). In rescuing this child, the princess took a personal and political risk. The princess adopted the baby and named him after how she found him (v. 10). Since 'Moses' sounds like 'draw out' in Hebrew, his family may have had some input into his name."

The summary result of this risk is recorded in Hebrews 11:23-29 (NKJV), "By faith Moses, when he was born, was hidden three months by his parents, because they saw he was a beautiful child; and they were not afraid of the king's command. By faith Moses, when he became of age, refused to be called the son of Pharaoh's daughter, choosing rather to suffer affliction with the people of God than to enjoy the passing pleasures of sin, esteeming the reproach of Christ greater riches than the treasures in Egypt; for he looked to the reward. By faith he forsook Egypt, not fearing the wrath of the king; for he endured as seeing Him who is invisible. By faith he kept the Passover and the sprinkling of blood, lest he who destroyed the firstborn should touch them. By faith they passed through the Red Sea as by dry land, whereas the Egyptians, attempting to do so, were drowned…" There is a cliché that sometimes has value, namely: "We know not what the future holds but we know Who holds the future." This surely was a truism in the birth and life of Moses and as it was in the birth, escape and life of Jesus Christ. To be secured in the hollow of God's hand and to be kept in the center of His will is one's safest place for His follower to be. Are you confident that, positionally, you are in this kind of relationship with the Lord?

In the parable of The Lost Sheep, Matthew 18:10-14 (NIV), Jesus makes special reference to the "little ones" and how one should treat them, as well as an eternal consequence for those who fail to do so. Note what Jesus teaches: "See that you do not despise one of these little ones. For I tell you that in heaven their angels always see the face of my Father who is in heaven. What do you think? If a man has a hundred sheep, and one of them has gone astray, does he not leave the ninety-nine on the mountains and go in search of the one that went astray? And if he finds it, truly, I say to you, he rejoices over it more than over the ninety-nine that never went astray. So it is not the will of my Father who is in heaven that one of these little ones should perish." Jesus is not speaking of sheep but children. Matthew 18:2-6 (NKJV) establishes that Jesus is teaching a lesson about humility and how a child is a visible example of that reality. Remember what Jesus did, "And calling to him a child, he put him in the midst of them…" He goes on to emphasize, "…whoever humbles himself like this child…" He then underscores, "Whoever receives one such child in my name receives me…" and goes on to indicate the consequence for both ignoring this teaching and disregarding "one of these little ones" with the words, "…whoever causes one of these little ones who believe in me to sin, it would be better for him to have a great millstone fastened around his neck and to be drowned in the depth of the sea." The words of Jesus are clear and intense. The severity of the condemnation is indicative of the importance of children in the ministry of Jesus and as a continuing example for the follower of Jesus Christ. He wants His people to have a special regard for all of the "little ones". They are precious in His sight and He wants them to be precious in your sight as well. This is equally true for the "little boats and little people" who are a real part of our everyday lives. Do you see them? Do you endeavor to know them? Do you attempt to be a positive influence that will impact their safety and well-being?

APPLICATION and QUESTIONS:

What did Jesus intend when He said you must humble yourself as a little child?

As and if you do so, what will that look like, and how will it affect and/or impact someone else?

The children who you see and know, do you value them as being part of the heritage of God?

As a "biblical Christian" and as one who is part of the household of God, what interest and involvement do you have with the "little boats, little people and little lambs" who are part of the Christian community or the neighborhood where you reside?

With the number of abortions, and the increasing number of child abuse cases, is there something that you should be doing, such as, speaking in behalf of those who cannot speak for themselves? How and where would you do this?

Are you able to intercede in behalf of the unwanted and abandoned child or the abused and aborted child and to do so without any fanfare or desire for acclaim or recognition? In other words, can you do so as you walk humbly with God?

Are you aware of anyone within your circle of acquaintances who could benefit from your involvement and participation in their life?

Will you take the next step and become involved in such a life?

Are you willing to implement Proverbs 31:9, "Open your mouth, judge righteously, and plead the cause of the poor and needy?"

And all of you, serve each other in humility,
for God sets himself against the proud,
but he shows favor to the humble.
So humble yourselves under the mighty power of God,
and in his good time he will honor you.
I Peter 5:5-6, *The New Living Translation*

4. A Serious Reminder

Events in our world occur more rapidly than one is able to comprehend or imagine. If times are difficult for those with some ability to adjust to uncertain economic conditions, as well as any shift towards socialism (or worse), what about the "little boats, little people and other sheep" who had little or nothing to begin with, and who are well below many on the economic ladder? If it may prove to be difficult to help oneself, what word of hope and faith does one have to share with the "little boats, little people and other sheep?" These are the ones who are closest to the vortex and who have little strength to escape being sucked down to certain devastation?

An example of an event that saw a rapid shift in standards and practice is evidenced by the Roe V. Wade decision in 1973 that legalized abortion on demand. Within a forty-year window, more than fifty-four million babies have been aborted. Shortly after that court decision, two men (in 1979), Dr. Frances A. Schaeffer and Dr. C. Everett Koop, toured this country and conducted seminars on the theme of: "Whatever Happened To The Human Race?" A subordinate title states: "Exposing Our Rapid Yet Subtle Loss of Human Rights." An introductory summary about their book with that title indicates, "Francis Schaeffer and former Surgeon General C. Everett Koop deal directly with the devaluing of human life and its results in our society. It did not take place in a vacuum. It is a direct result of a worldview that has rejected the doctrine of man being created in the image of God. Man as a product of the impersonal, plus time and chance has no sufficient basis for worth." The concern of these men appears in their statement, "The thinkables of the eighties and nineties will certainly include things which most people today find unthinkable and immoral, even unimaginable and too extreme to suggest. Yet – since they do not have some overriding principle that takes them beyond relativistic thinking – when these become thinkable and acceptable in the eighties and nineties, most people will not even remember that they were unthinkable in the seventies. They will slide into each new thinkable without a jolt." These two men were "prophets" to a previous generation as well as to ours.

One other important statement contained in chapter one of their book states, "...because the Christian consensus has been put aside, we are faced today with a flood of personal cruelty. As we have noted, the Christian consensus gave great freedoms without leading to chaos because society in general functioned within the values given in the Bible, especially the unique value of human life. Now that Humanism has taken over, the former freedoms run riot, and individuals, acting on what they are taught, increasingly practice their cruelties without restraint. And why shouldn't they? If the modern humanistic view of man is correct and man is only a product of chance in a universe that has no ultimate values, why should an individual refrain from being cruel to another person, if that person seems to be standing in his or her way?" Since that was true in 1979, what would their commentary be about our day and time? How much greater would they assess the decline just a generation later?

In chapter three, entitled, "Death By Someone's Choice," they write, "Life is a continuum from conception until natural death. Since life is being destroyed before birth, why not tamper with it on the other end? Will a society which has assumed the right to kill infants in the womb, because they are unwanted, imperfect, or merely inconvenient, have difficulty in assuming the right to kill other human beings, especially older adults who are judged unwanted, deemed imperfect physically or mentally, or considered a possible social nuisance? The next candidates for arbitrary reclassification as nonpersons are the elderly. This will become increasingly so as the proportion of the old and weak in relation to the young and strong becomes abnormally large. The imbalance will cause many of the young to perceive the old as a cramping nuisance in the hedonistic life-style they claim as their right..." What will society offer as an alternative? How does one go about determining and orchestrating a desired result? Some of the historic methods have been abortion, infanticide, euthanasia, ethnic-cleansing, genocide and population control. There are laws that govern the number and gender of children who can be born (an example is the nation of China), and whatever else a debased and evil mind can devise.

Reuters reported in June 2011 that, "...an example of one who championed euthanasia ('death with dignity') was "Assisted suicide advocate Jack Kevorkian, known as 'Dr. Death' for having helped more than 100 people end their lives...Kevorkian, a pathologist, was focused on death and dying long before he ignited a polarizing national debate over assisted suicide by crisscrossing Michigan in a rusty Volkswagen van hauling a machine to help sick and suffering people end their lives. Some viewed him as a hero who allowed the terminally ill to die with dignity, while his harshest critics reviled him as a cold-blooded killer who preyed on those suffering from chronic pain and depression. Most of his clients were middle-aged women. Kevorkian launched his assisted-suicide campaign in 1990, allowing an Alzheimer's patient to kill herself using a machine he devised that allowed her to trigger a lethal drug injection. He was charged with first-degree murder in the case, but the charges were later dismissed..."

In our nation, the Affordable Health Care Act was approved by a majority vote in the United States Senate (60 to 39) on December 24, 2009. Many people have expressed a concern over what will occur in terms of their personal health care needs. The suspicion arises from some of the detail written in the Affordable Health Care Act that calls for, and will allow for "...a panel of bureaucrats who have the power to make life and death decisions about health care funding. It's called the Independent Payment Advisory Board (IPAB) and its purpose is to keep costs down by actually denying care via price controls and inefficient bureaucracy. The IPAB will create a 15-member panel of health experts, appointed by the President and confirmed by the United States Senate." According to an essay in the New England Journal of Medicine, "the panel will be charged with ensuring that Medicare Expenses stay within limits set by the healthcare reform law, and must also recommend to Congress how to control healthcare costs."

Will a panel of people be appointed who will regulate and control when and where one can have medical care and procedures? It appears that is a distinct likelihood. Taking it a step further, will this be a "death panel" as some suggest and fear making a decision whether or not any care or procedure will be approved for one desiring and needing it? By adding millions of Medicare patients who have not had medical provision previously, the likelihood is present that there will be delays, inordinate delays, that could preclude someone might die before medical care or procedures can be approved and scheduled. If this is decided by other factors, such as the age of the patient or the presumed quality of life of a person, that could also bring about the worst fears into the realm of reality.

If times like these become the reality in one's life, are there any biblical directives that can serve as a guideline? Is there any way to bring encouragement and hope for those who have no voice that will be heard and little or no means by which they can be sustained? What about the "little boats, little people and other sheep" drifting through this world and system, what will happen to them? If everything should suddenly fail, what can one do? The biblical Christian has reminders throughout the Word of God that God is faithful and will never forsake His own. We should never allow our "what ifs" to short-circuit our trust and confidence in the faithful

God. There were difficult times before and there will be again. That is not a fatalistic view of the world but the reality. This may be the reason why in Psalm 20:7-8 the Psalmist wrote, "Some trust in chariots, and some in horses; but we will remember the name of the Lord our God. They have bowed down and fallen; but we have risen and stand upright." The application is that one's strength and confidence is never in things but only and always in the Lord alone. One needs to remember this truth and be reassured of God's presence and faithfulness.

Habakkuk was a prophet who lived in desperate times. He lived and ministered in the mid-seventh century BC. Looming on his horizon was Babylon with all of its force and military designs. They would soon lay siege upon and capture Jerusalem. Much will be destroyed and many will be taken away into captivity. Habakkuk 1:2-4 (NKJV) is the beginning of a prayer dialogue between Habakkuk and the Lord. Habakkuk prays, "O Lord, how long shall I cry, And You will not hear? Even cry out to You, Violence! and You will not save. Why do You show me iniquity, and cause me to see trouble? For plundering and violence are before me; there is strife, and contention arises. Therefore the law is powerless, and justice never goes forth. For the wicked surround the righteous; therefore perverse judgment proceeds." Habakkuk is frustrated by the on-going trend of his day and his sense helplessness in terms of knowing what he, or anyone, can do about it.

Many times, when one prays, the response of the Lord is not always that which one anticipated or expected. The Lord's timing is not always in the immediate even though one's desire is for something to occur now, not later. When one prays, care must be exercised that one is seeking God's will and not dictating what "I" want at a given moment. The Lord responds in Habakkuk 1:5, "Look among the nations and watch. Be utterly astounded! For I will work a work in your days which you would not believe, though it were told you." In the twenty-first century, do we believe that the

Lord will hear and respond to our prayers? Do we believe that He is concerned and not aloof? One would do well to remember how the Lord has consistently reminded His people. First, a statement by the Lord that should cause all of His people to be encouraged and have hope, Jeremiah 29:11-14 (NIV), "For I know the plans I have for you, declares the Lord, plans to prosper you and not to harm you, plans to give you hope and a future. Then you will call upon me and come and pray to me, and I will listen to you. You will seek me and find me when you seek me with all your heart. I will be found by you, declares the Lord…" Do we believe He has a perfect plan for our lives and His creation? Are we willing for our lives to be fitted into His will and plan for them?

There is a similar statement of encouragement and hope in Romans 8:28-31 (NIV), "And we know that in all things God works for the good of those who love him, who have been called according to his purpose…What…shall we say in response to this? If God is for us, who can be against us?" Paul goes on to ask and answer an important question for the biblical Christian in Romans 8:35-37 (NIV), "Who shall separate us from the love of Christ? Shall trouble or hardship or persecution or famine or nakedness or danger or sword? … No, in all these things we are more than conquerors through him who loved us." Don't look and dwell on your circumstances, but rather look to the Lord and rest in His promises. He knows who you are and where you are. He knows what you need and when you need it. One has correctly suggested, "don't look at yourself as a victim, but as a victor." How do you see yourself, a victim or a victor?

In the Sermon on the Mount, Jesus took considerable time to reassure His followers of the eternal plan and the practical provisions for His children. In Matthew 6:25-34 (NIV), Jesus shares with His disciples how God knows our needs and will meet those needs in ways that one cannot fathom or predict. He said, "Do not worry about your life, what you will eat or drink; or about your body, what you will wear. Is not life more important than food, and the body more important than clothes? ... Who of you by worrying can add a single hour to his life? ... And why do you worry about clothes? See how the lilies of the field grow. They do not labor or spin. Yet I tell you that not even Solomon in all his splendor was dressed like one of these. If that is how God clothes the grass of the field, which is here today and tomorrow is thrown into the fire, will he not much more clothe you, O you of little faith? So do not worry, saying, What shall we eat? or What shall we drink? or What shall we wear? Your heavenly Father knows that you need them. But seek first his kingdom and his righteousness, and all these things will be given to you as well. Therefore do not worry..." The word "worry" and the word "anxiety" are interchanged in the various translations. However, the message is the same, namely, don't be wringing your hands in despair over matters your Father in heaven has already taken care of for you. In His time, at just the right and appropriate time, His provision will be made available to and for you.

In some way, Habakkuk discerned these principles in the message of Jesus, and following his extended dialogue with God in prayer, he came to a profound conclusion in Habakkuk 3:13-18 (NIV), "You came out to deliver your people, to save your anointed one. You crushed the leader of the land of wickedness, you stripped him from head to foot...With his own spear you pierced his head when his warriors stormed out to scatter us, gloating as though about to devour the wretched who were in hiding. You trampled the sea with your horses, churning the great waters. I heard and my heart pounded, my lips quivered at the sound; decay crept into my bones, and my legs trembled. Yet I will wait patiently for the day of calamity to come on the nation invading us. Though the fig tree does not bud and there are no grapes on the vines, though the olive crop fails and the fields produce no food, though there are no sheep in the pen and no cattle in the stalls, yet I will rejoice in the Lord, I will be joyful in God my Savior. The Sovereign Lord is my strength; he makes my feet like the feet of a deer, he enables me to go on the heights."

Habakkuk is assured, that even if he has nothing, he has the Lord God and therefore he has everything that he will ever need. Many times, being at zero, with nothing in hand and no resources remaining, it is at such a time that the Lord gains one's attention and where He can demonstrate that He is all that one needs. A Hymn by an unknown author reminds one of this great truth about God, the Lord: Jesus Christ is ALL I Need.

> Jesus Christ is made to me, All I need, all I need,
> He alone is all my plea, He is all I need.
>
> He redeemed me when He died, All I need, all I need,
> I with Him was crucified, He is all I need.
>
> He's the treasure of my soul, All I need, all I need,
> He hath cleansed and made me whole, He is all I need.
>
> Jesus is my all in all, All I need, all I need,
> While He keeps I cannot fall, He is all I need.
> Glory, Glory to the Lamb, All I need, all I need,
> By His Spirit sealed I am, He is all I need.
> Refrain:
> Wisdom, righteousness and power, Holiness this very hour
> My redemption full and free, He is all I need.

APPLICATION and QUESTIONS:

What is your greatest "fear, worry, anxiety" at this time?

What about the trends and policies in our nation, do they concern and worry you? Is the government of men more powerful than God, the Creator of all?

What about the immediate and near future, if the political situation seems to be unable to function in a practical way, what do you view as your primary alternative? Why?

If everything that is dear to you is seized, confiscated, and/or destroyed, will that also remove the protective shield of God over His own? Will that eliminate the steady flow of His provision to meet your need?

When the children of Israel wandered in the wilderness, what did they have to do to receive God's provision for them?

Did they need that provision to survive?

What happened when they decided to take extra provision and hold it in reserve for a later time? Was that a wise move on their part? Why? Read Exodus 16:19-21 to assist you with your answer.

Is the message of Jesus in the Sermon on the Mount about "worry" and "anxiety" regarding the basics of life, applicable and workable for God's people today? Why? Why not?

> *Worrying is carrying tomorrow's load with today's strength*
> *- carrying two days at once.*
> *It is moving into tomorrow ahead of time.*
> *Worrying doesn't empty tomorrow of its sorrow,*
> *it empties today of its strength.*
> Corrie Ten Boom

5. A Serious Test

Testing is a very real part of one's life and experience. From time spent in school and into life experiences, tests and testing are present in various forms. In things we accept and take for granted, countless tests have been performed and revamping done before any of us gained first-hand knowledge or use of them. The cars one drives and the planes in which one flies have all been tested extensively to determine their safety and practical use. Many times, it is common-place to forget how the things we utilize came into being. Most are far-removed from the actual process that determines the usefulness of a product or mode of transportation. Perhaps that's a reason for the sense of surprise and bewilderment when such trials, hardships and difficulties occur. The difficulty occurs internally as one seeks to gain understanding of the why and how of these events and circumstances. These times do not just impact the "little boats or little people or other sheep." They are common place for everyone at some time and in some place.

Just because the common place can be anticipated at some point in life, one should never consider the tests of life as a time of rejection by the Lord but as a time of refinement and future blessing. An old hymn of the Church is, "How Firm A Foundation." One of the stanzas contains a perspective one should have regardless of the tests, trials, hardships, difficulties:

> When through fiery trials thy pathways shall lie,
> My grace, all sufficient, shall be thy supply;
> The flame shall not hurt thee; I only design
> Thy dross to consume, and thy gold to refine.

5. A Serious Test

A key phrase for our encouragement and edification is, "My Grace, all sufficient, shall be thy supply…" This should be a vital part of your core values, namely, the all-sufficient grace of God that sustains and supplies is sufficient for you! It is unlimited and unrestricted. It is the truth heard and embraced by The Apostle Paul when he prayed that the thorn in his flesh would be removed. The request of Paul and the answer given to him by the Lord, along with Paul's response, is given in II Corinthians 12:7-10 (NIV), "To keep me from becoming conceited because of these surpassingly great revelations, there was given me a thorn in my flesh, a messenger of Satan, to torment me. Three times I pleaded with the Lord to take it away from me. But he said to me, My grace is sufficient for you, for my power is made perfect in weakness. Therefore I will boast all the more gladly about my weaknesses, so that Christ's power may rest on me. That is why, for Christ's sake, I delight in weaknesses, in insults, in hardships, in persecutions, in difficulties. For when I am weak, then I am strong." How best can you apply this fact to your life today? How can you encourage the "little boats, little people and other sheep" with these truths you have embraced and believe?

There are several other biblical narratives that address the trials of life and the presence of God and His grace. One interesting statement is in Psalm 73:1-16 *(The Message)*, "No doubt about it! God is good - good to good people, good to the good-hearted. But I nearly missed it, missed seeing his goodness. I was looking the other way, looking up to the people at the top, envying the wicked who have it made, who have nothing to worry about, not a care in the whole wide world. Pretentious with arrogance, they wear the latest fashions in violence, pampered and overfed, decked out in silk bows of silliness. They jeer, using words to kill; they bully their way with words. They're full of hot air, loudmouths disturbing the peace. People actually listen to them - can you believe it? Like thirsty puppies, they lap up their words. What's going on here? Is God out to lunch? Nobody's tending the store. The wicked get by with everything; they have it made, piling up riches I've been stupid to play by the rules; what has it gotten me? A long run of bad luck, that's what - a slap in the face every time I walk out the door. If I'd have given in and talked like this, I would have betrayed your dear children. Still, when I tried to figure it out, all I got was a splitting headache." Have you ever felt this way? Have you thought that your best efforts for the Lord were in vain? Do you think He may have forgotten you?

Well, the Psalmist did. He goes on to say in verses 17-28 (*The Message*), "I felt neglected and overlooked until I entered the sanctuary of God. Then I saw the whole picture: The slippery road you've put them on, with a final crash in a ditch of delusions. In the blink of an eye, disaster! A blind curve in the dark, and - nightmare! We wake up and rub our eyes…Nothing. There's nothing to them. And there never was. When I was beleaguered and bitter, totally consumed by envy, I was totally ignorant, a dumb ox in your very presence. I'm still in your presence, but you've taken my hand. You wisely and tenderly lead me, and then you bless me. You're all I want in heaven! You're all I want on earth! When my skin sags and my bones get brittle, God is rock-firm and faithful. Look! Those who left you are falling apart! Deserters, they'll never be heard from again. But I'm in the very presence of God - oh, how refreshing it is! I've made Lord God my home. God, I'm telling the world what you do!" In which half of Psalm 73 do you see yourself? Are you in the first half, failing the tests of life or in the second half, rejoicing in the reality of being in the presence of the Lord continually?

Aging can bring with it a whole bevy of new experiences. There will be aches and pains and a general reduction in productive output. The inner self and drive wants to keep up the pace from younger days but the time-clock in one's body suggests otherwise. When Julie Andrews turned age seventy, there was a unique public moment that was shared. "To commemorate her birthday, actress/vocalist, Julie Andrews made a special appearance at

Manhattan's Radio City Music Hall for the benefit of the AARP. One of the musical numbers she performed was "My Favorite Things" from the legendary movie, *The Sound Of Music*. Some of the lyrics she used at that celebration are:

> Botox and nose drops and needles for knitting,
> Walkers and handrails and new dental fittings...
> Pacemakers, golf carts and porches with swings,
> These are a few of my favorite things.
> When the pipes leak, When the bones creak,
> When the knees go bad,
> I simply remember my favorite things,
> And then I don't feel so bad...
> When the joints ache, When the hips break,
> When the eyes grow dim,
> Then I remember the great life I've had,
> And then I don't feel so bad.

On a more serious note, The Apostle Paul shares his frustration because of a malady that he felt was hindering his productivity (II Corinthians 12:7-10 - NIV). Part of that account is shared in *Today In The Word*, for June 28, 2012 and entitled: "God Allows Bodily Suffering." "When diagnosed with a brain disorder, the response of one Christian woman was what few would have imagined. Moved not by her prognosis but by a confidence in God's faithfulness, she mused, 'The Lord is definitely letting me experience His strength as we begin this new journey.' Anticipating surgery, she prayed, 'Thank you, Jesus, for the opportunity to turn my whole life over to you and trust that you are walking—and sometimes carrying—me through each day.' Her attitude was shared by the apostle Paul. In this letter to the church in Corinth, Paul addresses some of their attacks on his leadership. Though he defended both his credentials and his authority, Paul did confess what he called 'a thorn in my flesh' (v. 7). This phrase is also used in Numbers 33:55, and it suggested then just what it does today: 'an irksome annoyance!' The particular nature of Paul's 'thorn' has been debated over the centuries. Was it spiritual or physical? Sixteenth-century reformers Martin Luther and John Calvin believed Paul's thorn to be a temptation to unbelief. Others have assumed it to be a physical malady. Still others have guessed Paul was referring to having a hot temper. This is all speculation, because Scripture does not tell us. Though we can't identify the particularities of Paul's thorn, the context of this passage does make one thing clear, it was a weakness. The Lord spoke into that thorny situation, saying, 'My grace is sufficient for you, for my power is made perfect in weakness' (v. 9). In Paul's life, and in ours, the point or moment of our greatest weakness is when Christ's power is most clearly revealed."

Rather than praying any further about his need, and instead of grumbling or complaining about it, he arrived at a point of resolve. We need to share in that sense of God's power in us and His provision for us. We need to move beyond a theoretical faith that allows us to "believe that God is able" to a practical faith that allows us to say and "believe that God is not only able, but that He will!" It is the faith that sustained three young men as they faced a sentence of death administered by King Nebuchadnezzar, Daniel 3:16-18 (NIV). To avoid the death sentence, all they had to do was to compromise their core values. Given that opportunity, they refused. "Shadrach, Meshach and Abednego replied to the king, "O Nebuchadnezzar, we do not need to defend ourselves before you in this matter. If we are thrown into the blazing furnace, the God we serve is able to save us from it, and he will rescue us from your hand, O king. But even if he does not, we want you to know, O king, that we will not serve your gods or worship the image of gold you have set up." Their confidence was clear when they confidently asserted: "...the God we serve is able to save us from it, and he will rescue us from your hand..." It was a classic example of the standard that God's people should affirm: No Compromise and No Surrender!

Paul shares a very meaningful prayer for the believers at Ephesus. In Ephesians 3:14-21 (NIV), Paul writes and prays: "...I kneel before the Father, from whom his whole family in heaven and on earth derives its name. I pray that out of his glorious riches he may strengthen you with power through his Spirit in your inner being, so that Christ may dwell in your hearts through faith. And I pray that you, being rooted and established in love, may have power, together with all the saints, to grasp how wide and long and high and deep is the love of Christ, and to know this love that surpasses knowledge, that you may be filled to the measure of all the fullness of God. Now to him who is able to do immeasurably more than all we ask or imagine, according to his power that is at work within us, to him be glory in the church and in Christ Jesus throughout all generations, for ever and ever! Amen." He emphasizes the power of God in the believer and the power of God that will "...do immeasurably more than all we ask or imagine, according to His power that is at work in us..." Do you have an understanding of and appreciation for the power of God that is available to you and for you every moment of every day?

This truth about the power of God has somehow been removed from the thinking and practice of many. The "little boats or little people or other sheep" might be willing to turn to this source of power, but too often, they have not witnessed it as a professing Christian's belief system or practice. How does this impact the "little boat, little people and other sheep" when they find themselves in dire straits and circumstances? If the Church fails to live by the truth of God's power at work in us, what alternative is left for people? For many years, it appears that the government at all levels has been willing to step into that vacuum and use tax dollars to meet needs (and maybe, use that assistance as a means of securing votes for elective office). Currently, in the United States of America, it is estimated that one-third of the population, more than 100 million people, are receiving welfare benefits from the Federal Government. Approximately forty-three million people receive Food Stamps on a regular basis; and with the continuing rate of high unemployment, many have given up looking for a job and have filed for disability payments instead. With a federal deficit at a level of eighteen trillion-dollars and growing, and industry locating outside of the United States, along with the high numbers of unemployed and under-employed, and the considerable number on the welfare rolls, the present and future for many looks bleak at best and dismal at worst.

The biblical Christian must be different. He/She must be a beacon of light as a representative of The One who came and declared, "I AM the Light of the world..." The "little boats" need to be shone a path through the darkness so they can come to the Light. The "little people" need to emulate an example that they can see and follow that will enable them to find The One who declared, "I Am the Bread of Life..." and have their needs met by Him. The "other sheep" need to be led to the Shepherd so they can hear His voice and follow Him (John 10:27-30). Those who are enduring affliction and pain need to see some glimmer of hope that will bring them to the Great Physician. Is your life a beacon of light that causes people to head in the direction of The True Light? One's "faith" should never be viewed by others as being only theoretical. They must be able to see the practical reality of it by one's lifestyle and daily walk. Remember the words of the refrain to the hymn: "What You Are":

> What you are speaks so loud that the world can't hear what you say;
> They're looking at your walk, not listening to your talk,
> They're judging from your actions every day.
> Don't believe you'll deceive

5. A Serious Test

> By claiming what you've never know
> They'll accept what they see and know you to be,
> They'll judge from your life alone.

Some people one encounters will be doing their best to cope with pain. For some, it is intense. For others, while it causes difficulty and restriction, they are doing their best to manage their pain. The John Ankerberg Show has done valuable work on the subject of pain and physical adversity. Several examples are used of people, some well-known, who have seen their pain and restriction in terms of the eternal purpose of God. One example given is Dr. John MacArthur, who survived a car crash, and saw that as a means of God getting his attention and ultimately into ministry. He wrote: "Romans 8:28 is absolutely a comprehensive statement. There are no caveats, there are no exceptions. Good things work together for our good. Bad things work together for our good. Neutral things work together for our good…suffering works together for our good and struggling with temptation works together for our good. Even sin [is something that] God causes to work together for our good by overruling it for our present benefit and our ultimate glory. No statement made to a believer could contribute more hope, more happiness, more freedom and more joy in the heart than that statement because what it says is that no matter what pain, no matter what problems, no matter what failures, no matter what difficulties, no matter what disasters, no matter what sin, no matter what suffering, no matter what temptation, all things work together for good… It is a comprehensive promise. And the context has no limits, the context puts no limits on it. There's nothing that qualifies the 'all things,' nothing. It means absolutely what it says, all things work together for good for those who love the Lord who are called according to his purpose. God takes anything and everything that occurs in a believer's life and rather than it potentiating the believer's loss of salvation, rather than it potentiating the believer's condemnation, God makes it work together for the believer's ultimate good. This is the greatest promise that we can have in this life. There are absolutely no limits on this statement in this context. It is limitless."

In terms of how this promise in Romans 8:28 works, Dr. MacArthur goes on to say: "As long as something is in harmony with God's nature and attributes, nothing is impossible with God, as Scripture clearly teaches (Genesis 18:14): 'Is anything too hard for the Lord?' Jeremiah also declared, 'Nothing is too hard for you' (Jeremiah 32:7). Jesus said, 'For nothing is impossible with God' (Luke 1:37). Romans 8:28 is clearly a promise of God. Further, please observe that God does not want His children to have the slightest doubt in the matter because the verse begins His promise with "we know…"

Thomas C. Black wrote and posted a poem on his webpage – StillTruth.com - reminding the biblical Christian of one's source of victory, namely, God Alone.

> God grants the Victory!
> The Cross proclaims His righteousness -
> The empty tomb shouts His glory.
>
> God has the Victory!
> The tears of saints entreat His hand -
> The prayerful cry of the righteous echoes His praise.
>
> God is the Victory!
> Every power is beneath His power –
> The evil will see it and shudder.
>
> God gives the Victory!
> The empty tomb shouts His victory –
> The blood-stained cross provides our peace.

5. A Serious Test

> To the repentant one sins are forgiven!
> To the dependent one heaven's throne bends its ears –
> God grants the Victory!

A foundational truth of our faith and practice is I Corinthians 15:57 (NKJV), "Thanks be to God Who gives us the victory through our Lord Jesus Christ."

APPLICATION and QUESTIONS:

When you are confronted with a test or trial, what is your first response, secular or spiritual?

What do you believe is the purpose of a test or trial that comes your way?

If you have a major accident or injury, what is your first thought?

In terms of Faith and Practice, what are three of the first principles that should be engaged when you experience an injury or other physical need?

If you've tried to do right and seemingly failed, what should you do next?

Do you find it easier to tell others what they should do and how they should live than it is for you to be a model that can be emulated?

If there was one "failure" situation that you could try to do differently, what would it be? In retrospect, how might it have been avoided?

How often should one rehearse his/her failures to others? What goal is in view if this has been your practice?

Nothing is impossible when you put your trust in God;
Nothing is impossible when you're trusting in His Word.
Hearken to the voice of God to thee;
"Is there anything too hard for Me?"
Then put your trust in God alone and rest upon His Word;
For everything, O, everything, yes everything is possible with God.

Eugene L. Clark

6. A Serious Strategy

There is an old saying that states, "If you aim at nothing, you will always hit your target." Some may remember the time when Charlie Brown was about to practice archery with his bow and arrow. In order to attain "Flawless Execution" by hitting the bullseye with each arrow, he developed a unique method. The story line is: "One day Charlie Brown was in his backyard having target practice with his bow and arrows. He would pull the bow string back and let the arrow fly into a fence. Then he would go to where the arrow had landed and draw a target around it. Several arrows and targets later, Lucy said to Charlie Brown, you don't have target practice that way. You draw the target, then shoot the arrow. Charlie Brown responded, I know that, but if you do it my way, you never miss!" In fiction, Charlie Brown could almost be the poster person for the ideal of the "little boats, little people and other sheep". He was innocent, trusting, desiring acceptance, but all too often he was treated as one who was gullible or inconsequential. While many might identify with a Charlie Brown character, life is not that simple. While Charlie Brown had his failures, such as letting Lucy hold the football while he tried to kick it, he was able to maintain his innocence and readiness to try again.

In real life, an example of the tension between failure and success was Thomas A. Edison. While one benefits from some of his inventions, such as the electric light bulb, he was the holder of 1093 patents, many of which never came to fruition. His philosophy of life and his view of failure are summed up in quotes attributed to him, such as: Overcoming Failure: (1) "I am not discouraged, because every wrong attempt discarded is another step forward." (2) "I have not failed. I've just found 10,000 ways that won't work." (3) "Many of life's failures are men who did not realize how close they were to success when they gave up." In terms of effort required and necessary, he said: "Genius is one percent inspiration and ninety-nine percent perspiration." He also said, "The three great essentials to achieving anything worthwhile are; first, hard work, second, stick-to-it-ive-ness, and third, common sense." Quotes are informative about someone's philosophy of life and their work ethic. They can be valuable and useful to the one who is willing to take these quotes and incorporate them into his or her personal lifestyle, motivation and purpose.

The *Ladies' Home Journal*, September 2005, contained an article by Rick Warren about, "Failure Versus Success." He told of setting out with his family on an unplanned vacation trip. There was no specific destination and no advanced motel reservations. The idea was to just go, without any confining schedule or deadline, and stop where and when they were ready to do so. That was the plan. Each night when they tried to stop at a motel, they were told there were no rooms available. The result was that they had to sleep in the car. Near the end of the trip, finding a place to stay with his family was just one frustration after another. He recounts, "These episodes continued every night throughout our vacation until the last night on our last stop returning home. There I was, and there I sat in a loud and smoky Las Vegas hotel lobby at one in the morning, waiting for someone, anyone, to check out of the hotel so we could get a room. I sat there tired and agitated, thinking: 'Boy, what a big mistake this was, what a total failure.' Then I remembered what Thomas Edison had said: 'Don't call it a failure. Call it an education.' From that point of view, the vacation was extremely educational." Rick Warren continued as he shared his further thoughts about failure: "…nobody wants to be considered a failure. I began to think, if I fail, what will happen to me? What will other people think? Will I be considered worthless? Will anybody love me? We need never fear failure for two reasons: (1) God uses it to redirect us…Failure often forces us to reevaluate what's important in life… (2) Failure can develop our character…If we were to instantly succeed at everything we did, we'd become complacent, self-absorbed, arrogant and lazy…"

Have you ever had times it your life when you felt you were moving from one frustration to another, from one failure to another? Have you wondered why, and what you might choose to do because of it? In one of his Minister's Seminars, I recall Howard Hendricks asking the question: "What does it take to make you want to quit?" He wasn't advocating "quitting" but rather "perseverance." It seems as though "patience" and "perseverance" are joined together as character issues for each one. Does one have the desire and fortitude to seek patience and perseverance from the Lord? If the answer is "Yes," then there is a process by which one can learn, know and grow in patience and perseverance. One needs to be certain this is the desire, purpose and goal of one's life. The old saying, "Be careful what you ask for" is applicable here because the process is arduous and the result is seldom immediate. An insight into this process begins in Romans 5:1-5 (NKJV), "Therefore, having been justified by faith, we have peace with God through our Lord Jesus Christ, through whom also we have access by faith into this grace in which we stand, and rejoice in hope of the glory of God. And not only that, but we also glory in tribulations, knowing that tribulation produces perseverance; and perseverance, character; and character, hope. Now hope does not disappoint, because the love of God has been poured out in our hearts by the Holy Spirit who was given to us."

It is interesting to see the rendering of Romans 5:3-5 in *The Message Paraphrase*, "There's more to come: We continue to shout our praise even when we're hemmed in with troubles, because we know how troubles can develop passionate patience in us, and how that patience in turn forges the tempered steel of virtue, keeping us alert for whatever God will do next. In alert expectancy such as this, we're never left feeling shortchanged. Quite the contrary, we can't round up enough containers to hold everything God generously pours into our lives through the Holy Spirit!" The point being made is clear. Perseverance and patience come as the result of a process that will involve trials and troubles of one sort or another. It is a refining process that takes time until all of the junk and dross we've allowed to accumulate in our lives and thinking is purged away, and the new life in Christ's principles for our behavior are instilled and fully functional. If you want patience and perseverance, it will mean tribulation will be part of that journey and process.

Two other references are helpful to have in mind during this process. The first is John 16:31-33 (NKJV), "Jesus answered them, Do you now believe? Indeed the hour is coming, yes, has now come, that you will be scattered, each to his own, and will leave Me alone. And yet I am not alone, because the Father is with Me. These things I have spoken to you, that in Me you may have peace. In the world you will have tribulation; but be of good cheer, I have overcome the world." Jesus underscores two truths, (a) the reality of tribulation in one's life, and (b) we can always know His peace because He has overcome the world. Another reference to note is I Peter 4:12-14 (NKJV), "Beloved, do not think it strange concerning the fiery trial which is to try you, as though some strange thing happened to you; but rejoice to the extent that you partake of Christ's sufferings, that when His glory is revealed, you may also be glad with exceeding joy. If you are reproached for the name of Christ, blessed are you, for the Spirit of glory and of God rests upon you. On their part He is blasphemed, but on your part He is glorified." This, too, is part of the process, namely, fiery trials and suffering for Christ's sake.

In *the Matthew Henry Concise Commentary* on I Peter 4:12-19, we read: "By patience and fortitude in suffering, by dependence on the promises of God, and keeping to the word the Holy Spirit hath revealed, the Holy Spirit is glorified; but by the contempt and reproaches cast upon believers, he is evil spoken of, and is blasphemed. One would think such cautions as these were needless to Christians. But their enemies falsely charged them with foul crimes. And even the best of men need to be warned against the worst of sins. There is no comfort in sufferings, when we bring them upon ourselves by our own sin and folly. A time of universal calamity was at hand, as foretold by our Savior (Matthew 24:9-10). And if such things befall in this life, how awful will the day of judgment be! It is true that the righteous are scarcely saved; even those who endeavor to walk uprightly in the ways of God. This does not mean that the purposes…of God are uncertain, but only that great difficulties and hard encounters will be experienced as one goes through so many temptations and tribulations, so many fightings without and fears within. Yet all outward difficulties would be as nothing, were it not for lusts and corruptions within. These are the worst clogs and troubles. And if the way of the righteous be so hard, then how hard shall be the end of the ungodly sinner, who walks in sin with delight, and thinks the righteous is a fool for all his pains! The only way to keep the soul well is to commit it to God by prayer, and patient perseverance in well-doing. He will overrule all to the final advantage of the believer."

It is apparent that we are moving toward very difficult and trying times. As unbelievable and strange as it may appear, there are discussions and contingency plans being discussed in terms of an Insurrection in the United States. On Tuesday, August 7, 2012, *The Washington Times* published an editorial entitled, "The Civil War of 2016: U. S. Military Officers Are Told To Plan To Fight Americans." The scenario given and response to it is astonishing, and if true, is frightening. The scenario is, "Imagine Tea Party extremists seizing control of a South Carolina town and the Army being sent in to crush the rebellion. This farcical vision is now part of the discussion in professional military circles according to an article in the respected Small Wars Journal titled, "Full Spectrum Operations in the Homeland: A Vision of the Future." It was written by retired Army Col. Kevin Benson of the Army's University of Foreign Military and Cultural Studies at Fort Leavenworth, Kan., and Jennifer Weber, a Civil War expert at the University of Kansas. It posits an 'extremist militia motivated by the goals of the 'tea party' movement' seizing control of Darlington, S. C., in 2016, 'occupying City Hall, disbanding the city council and placing the mayor under house arrest.' The rebels set up checkpoints on Interstate 95 and Interstate 20 looking for illegal aliens. It's a cartoonish and needlessly provocative scenario. The article is a choppy patchwork of doctrinal jargon and liberal nightmare. The authors make a quasi-legal case for military action and then apply the Army's Operating Concept 2016-2028 to the situation. They write bloodlessly that 'once it is put into play, Americans will expect the military to execute without pause and as professionally as if it were acting overseas.' They claim that 'the Army cannot disappoint the American people, especially in such a moment,' not pausing to consider that using such efficient, deadly force against U. S. citizens would create a monumental political backlash and severely erode government legitimacy… The scenario presented in Small Wars Journal isn't a literary device but an operational lay-down intended to present the rationale and mechanisms for Americans to fight Americans. Col. Benson and Ms. Weber contend, 'Army officers are professionally obligated to consider the conduct of operations on U. S. soil.' This is a dark, pessimistic and wrongheaded view of what military leaders should spend their time studying…"

    When Peter wrote his epistle to the believers who were being scattered, Nero was the ruthless Ruler in Rome and issuing vicious and cruel edicts against the "elect who were scattered." This is not dissimilar from the actions during World War II against the Jews when more than six-million were persecuted, abused and executed. The ruthless and viciousness of dictators and leaders who want to gain and maintain power, and a stronghold over people, is often repeated and always difficult to comprehend. There's an interesting paragraph in the Book published in 2010 by Laura Hillenbrand titled, *Unbroken*. She is noted as "...one of our best writers of narrative history" (on the back jacket of the book). A summary states, "A World War II story of Survival, Resilience, and Redemption." There is a paragraph that addresses the manner in which Japan prepared itself to capture and control Asia and the Pacific. She writes (p. 43): "Japan's military-dominated government had long been preparing for its quest. Over decades, it had crafted a muscular technologically sophisticated army and navy, and through a military-run school system, that relentlessly and violently drilled children on the nation's imperial destiny, it had shaped its people for war. Finally, through intense indoctrination, beatings, and desensitization, its army cultivated and celebrated extreme brutality in its soldiers. Imbuing violence with holy meaning...the Japanese imperial army made violence a cultural imperative every bit as powerful as that which propelled Europeans during the Crusades and the Spanish Inquisition..." At the outset of the war in China, history indicates they carried out their objectives with cruelty, harsh treatment, lack of compassion and no mercy.

The secular world reminds us of the atrocities of the past and how they parallel similar inhumane treatment of people in the present. On August 9, 2012, the *Huffington Post* had an entry entitled, "Rwanda's Genocide and Lessons America Hasn't Learned for Syria." It is a re-focus upon the degree of genocide and how it was carried out. Just a couple of lines from the Editorial post: "...in April of 1994, approximately 5000 Tutsi men, women, and children had sought refuge in the Church to protect them from genocidal Hutu militiamen. But God sometimes hides and does not protect. After throwing grenades into the Church, the Hutu monsters axed, macheted, clubbed, and speared every last person to death. Today, their skulls, bones, coffins, and blood-soaked clothing decorate the Church in a macabre orgy of death...another Church, two hours away, where nearly 500 lime-preserved bodies, in their crouching postures of death, lie strewn around the Church after being found nearby in a mass grave. They remain there, unburied, silent witnesses to man's brutality to his fellow man... The American government...needs...to learn from the Rwandan experience and finally agree to put an end to mass slaughter and to seriously punish all those who engage in it. Why are we doing nothing in Syria? Why have 3.5 million people died of starvation in North Korea with barely an American response?"

In I Peter 4:12, the "fiery trial" might not just be the cruel action of a hostile, wicked and vicious political government, but rather the physical plight they were experiencing and the limitations under which they were compelled to live. In John Gill's Commentary on this verse, he writes: "...the apostle exhorts them not to look upon their afflictions that either did or should attend them as strange and uncommon things; since afflictions, of whatsoever kind, are not things of chance, and do not rise up out of the dust, but are by the appointment, and according to the will of God; and are also the common lot of the people of God in all ages, from the beginning of the world, the same afflictions are accomplished in others; yea, Christ himself endured the same hatred, reproach, and contradiction of sinners, against himself; and they are what he has given his people reason to expect, having told them of them before hand, that they might not be offended at them; and as they lay in his way to glory, it need not seem strange that the saints also should, through many tribulations, enter the kingdom. Moreover, this fiery dispensation, be it what it will, was not to destroy them, but to try them, and that for their good, profit, and advantage; just as gold and silver are tried in the fire, and lose their dross, and become purer and brighter..."

The point is that not all suffering or fiery trials will come at the hands of a wicked government of hostile forces. Some may occur by means of what is called an accident but in actuality may be for other reasons. Whatever the cause, one should exercise compassion, mercy and help for those who are enduring physical maladies, handicaps, and suffering. One's heart should never be calloused toward another. When we think of War, we should never forget the wounded warriors who have returned to their home and family suffering physical and mental issues. There should be concern for those with missing limbs who have a determination to strive for as much normalcy as they can, but who will need someone's help that will enable them to reach their goal. Those who will be unable to regain much physical functioning, need one's understanding and encouragement. They should not be forgotten or overlooked as though they were "little boats, little people or other sheep."

There are others who one minute were very active and athletic and the next minute were quadriplegics. There are several examples but one who is well-known is Joni Eareckson Tada. A brief biography states: "A diving accident in 1967 left Joni Eareckson, then 17, a quadriplegic in a wheelchair, unable to use her hands. After two years of rehabilitation, she emerged with new skills and a fresh determination to help others in similar situations. During her rehabilitation, Joni spent long months learning how to paint with a brush between her teeth. Her high-detail fine art paintings and prints are sought-after and collected. Her best-selling autobiography *Joni* and the feature film of the same name have been translated into many languages, introducing her to people around the world. She also has visited 46 countries. She has served on the National Council on Disability under President Reagan and President Bush and the Disability Advisory Committee to the U.S. State Department under Secretary of State Condoleezza Rice..." The John Ankerberg Website lists some of her other accomplishments that include: "...she has written some 100 books; become an accomplished painter, having painted over 150 pictures with her teeth, each one taking over a month; composed six music albums; is involved in 12 separate ministries she began with dozens of centers around the world; has helped people around the world in 25 different disability categories, including Wounded Warriors..." This and so much more amid the constancy of pain and limitations that could've easily caused others to give up and quit.

Michael J. Easley, former President of Moody Bible Institute, was a gifted and sought after minister and administrator. Wikipedia includes some biographical information: "...Before becoming president of Moody Bible Institute, Easley served as a pastor for twenty-four years, beginning as a youth pastor intern at Trinity Fellowship in Dallas, Texas. He then became senior pastor at Grand Prairie Bible Church in Texas, and then at Immanuel Bible Church in Springfield, Virginia, where he served for eleven and a half years. Since 1993, he and his wife have also spoken together at Family-Life Marriage Conferences. In the Summer of 2005, Easley became the president of Moody Bible Institute in Chicago, IL. He was the host of two radio programs sponsored by the Moody Bible Institute: Moody Presents and the 24-minute in Context, formerly a 15-minute program called Proclaim! The latter program debuted May 5, 2008. Easley wrote Interludes: Prayers And Reflections Of A Servant's Heart and contributed to The Da Vinci Code Controversy by Dillon Burroughs. He has also stood against The New International Version's gender inclusive language. On May 16, 2008, Easley submitted his resignation from Moody due to continuing back troubles, which he felt were impeding his abilities to be an effective president..." The pain was and is debilitating and most of his time he is confined to the use of a wheel chair. Like Joni Eareckson Tada, he has pressed on despite the constant pain and limitations.

One other example in the secular world is Charles Krauthammer. Part of his Biography is: "It was during his freshmen year in medical school that he had the accident that changed his life. He dove off the diving board at a swimming pool and hit his head on the bottom. Since then, he's been confined to a wheelchair, something few people know unless they've seen him in person or on television. While he was forced to make certain lifestyle changes, Krauthammer did not let the accident affect his ambition. He completed medical school and did a three year residency in psychiatry at Massachusetts General Hospital, serving as chief resident the last year. During that time he wrote a paper about a condition he called secondary mania. Almost twenty years later, one of Krauthammer's friends at the American Medical Association sent him a newsletter discussing the identification and treatment of secondary mania. I had said there was a disease no one recognized and gave it a name. I left the field before the paper was even published. I sent it in and then left. I discovered that an entire field of study had grown up around the paper. After all the hard work to become a physician, Krauthammer again decided that was not what he wanted to do..." He became a speech-writer for Walter Mondale, and also submitted some opinion columns to various publications. He has regularly appeared on the Fox News Network and National Public Television/Radio. Despite his obvious limitation, he is a sought-after commentator and presents his arguments logically and succinctly.

 To the best of one's ability and with the strength that the Lord provides for each new day, we need to implement Philippians 3:13-15 (NIV), "...one thing I do: forgetting what is behind and straining toward what is ahead, I press on toward the goal to win the prize for which God has called me heavenward in Christ Jesus. All of us who are mature should take such a view of things. And if on some point you think differently, that too God will make clear to you." *The Message Paraphrase* states these verses in plain and common language: "Friends, don't get me wrong: By no means do I count myself an expert in all of this, but I've got my eye on the goal, where God is beckoning us onward - to Jesus. I'm off and running, and I'm not turning back. So let's keep focused on that goal, those of us who want everything God has for us. If any of you have something else in mind, something less than total commitment, God will clear your blurred vision, you'll see it yet!" Some may no longer be able to run or walk, but the goal remains and one must press on to that goal.

Years ago, my wife and I were privileged to know a very dear soul. She had considerable physical limitations but every day she would manage to sit on her front porch with her Bible on her lap. She began her day with a prayer: "Lord, you have promised, As thy days, so shall they strength be. You have given me another day and I need Your strength to help me get through it." Then, she would spend quality time in The Word and Prayer, every day. She was a joy and delight to know. The words she prayed come from Deuteronomy 33:25-27 (NKJV). The Lord is speaking of Asher and says: "As your days, so shall your strength be. There is no one like the God of Jeshurun, Who rides the heavens to help you, and in His excellency on the clouds. The eternal God is your refuge, And underneath are the everlasting arms…" Let those words be your encouragement and the source of your strength. You should also look for opportunities to share these truths with the "little boats, little people and other sheep" who are so often downtrodden and treated as a nuisance. Let them know that The Lord values them and they are significant in His sight.

APPLICATION and QUESTIONS:

What primary and necessary quality does Charlie Brown epitomize and demonstrate? When you shoot your arrows, are you like Charlie Brown – painting the target around your arrow in the fence?

If Lucy inserted your name in her statement, would your response be the same as Charlie Brown's? ("Lucy said to Charlie Brown, you don't have target practice that way. You draw the target, then shoot the arrow. Charlie Brown responded, I know that, but if you do it my way, you never miss")? What goal(s) have you established for your life for today and all your future days?

Generally, what does it take to make you want to quit? Why?

How do you cope with the challenges that may be present in your life? Do you go into seclusion or do you press on to accomplish what you can while you can?

Does pain, or restriction, or malady overwhelm you and prevent you from being active? Why?

What if you suddenly became a quadriplegic similar to Joni Eareckson Tada and Charles Krauthammer? What if you were diving one minute and paralyzed almost immediately for the rest of your life? What would you see as a possibility and potential for your life?

Inasmuch as many of you reading these questions are not quadriplegics, what reason or excuse do you believe is valid if you have given up trying to be or making a difference?

What one Scripture passage can you embrace as part of your spiritual DNA and as a foundational principle for your life (Take a peek at Philippians 4:13 and 4:19 and see if that could be useful in giving you a jump-start!)? What Scripture passage would be on your list?

> *Who shall dare let his incapacity for hope or goodness*
> *cast a shadow upon the courage of those*
> *who bear their burdens as if they were privileges?*
>
> Helen Keller

7. A Serious Challenge

A previous chapter concluded with reference to some who deal with debilitating pain daily and/or who are quadriplegic. Their lives were suddenly and dramatically changed. They had two choices, either allow themselves to become totally immobile for the remainder of their lives, or make a calculated determination to do whatever they could with the remaining physical function they possessed. They could either wrap themselves in self-pity and seek sympathy for their plight, or they could determine what their potential for usefulness would be from this point forward and follow-through as best they could.

One man, who we will identify as Harry, lived a very interesting and fruitful life, even though a good portion of it was lived in a wheelchair. He was one who contracted polio and it left him largely immobile. One might suppose that Harry would view his plight negatively and live his life as an invalid. However, he had committed his life to the Lord and was willing to serve Him in whatever capacity he could. No task was too daunting for him and he offered no excuses. He did what he could to the best of his ability. As a result of his commitment and determination, the Lord enabled him to pioneer the start of two churches, and to see them flourish. I knew Harry and had occasion to visit with him but he never complained about his station in life. He was thankful to be alive and that the Lord was willing to use him in ministry. Harry is out of his wheelchair now and walking around heaven.

There was another man who we will identify as Tommy. He would not be known by too many people but he was loved and respected by those who took time to make his acquaintance. In some ways, he might even be thought of as one of the "little boats, little people or other sheep". Since he was a humble man, being

7. A Serious Challenge

thought of as a "little boat, little person or other sheep" would have been fine with him. Tommy had been very active and knew how to live a full life. One day, while driving his truck, he was involved in an accident and injured. From being very active, he was suddenly a paraplegic. What should he do? What could he do? Was there a place where he would be gainfully employed so he could support his family? There were many questions and no immediate answers. However, Tommy was not one who would be content to be an invalid, nor would he allow himself to vegetate on the sideline. He went on to become a counselor who worked with handicapped people. He transported himself in a Chevrolet El Camino that was equipped so he could drive it. It had a hoist and controls so he could get his wheelchair from the back of the El Camino to the driver's door for his use. He remained very active in secular employment as well as spiritual activity in his church. One of Tommy's commendable qualities was his unwillingness to offer an excuse or to beg-off of a responsibility. He could have easily done so and almost everyone would have understood. But, that was not Tommy. One example was when his church was doing evangelism. Names were assigned and visits were to be made. However, some were hesitant and timid about intruding into someone's home to evangelize. However, Tommy was different. He would call in advance and ask to be invited. He would then indicate that he would need their assistance so he could get up the steps into their home. Because of his manner and approach, most of the people he contacted agreed and he gained entrance. They gladly helped him up in his wheelchair. In these visits, he was privileged to lead several people to receive Jesus Christ as their Savior and Lord.

There was one other commendable quality of Tommy, namely, he did not treat anyone as though they were "little boats, little people, other sheep." Even though he was busy, he made time available to all. He was one who had a keen sense of someone's need and was gifted to discern the urgency of the moment. He would willingly interrupt what he had scheduled in an effort to minister to a life that needed ministering at that moment. One can only pray that his tribe would increase. He is now with the Lord and doubtlessly well-rewarded for his willingness and readiness to serve the Lord as best he could for as long as he could.

It is sad to see able-bodied people sitting on the sidelines and developing a personal list of excuses for the things they don't wish to do. They allow themselves to atrophy rather than gaining in strength by becoming actively engaged in the task of reaching out with concern for the souls of men. One of the possible definitions for excuse is: "a pretext or subterfuge." The making and offering of excuses is nothing new. There is an applicable parable of Jesus in Luke 14:17-24 (NIV), "At the time of the banquet he sent his servant to tell those who had been invited, Come, for everything is now ready. But they all alike began to make excuses. The first said, I have just bought a field, and I must go and see it. Please excuse me. Another said, I have just bought five yoke of oxen, and I'm on my way to try them out. Please excuse me. still another said, I just got married, so I can't come." The operative phrase is: "...they all alike began to make excuses..." Does that sound familiar and strike a chord? One can believe that his/her excuses are understood, valid and acceptable. Should such excuses be understood and acceptable within the body of Christ? Are they deemed valid by Jesus Christ who has assigned His body the responsibility to be engaged in the mission and task of reaching precious souls for Him?

The text in Luke 14:21-24 (NIV) indicates, "The servant came back and reported this to his master. Then the owner of the house became angry and ordered his servant, Go out quickly into the streets and alleys of the town and bring in the poor, the crippled, the blind and the lame. Sir, the servant said, what you ordered has been done, but there is still room. Then the master told his servant: Go out to the roads and country lanes and make them come in, so that my house will be full. I tell you, not one of those men who were invited will get a taste of my banquet." Excuses may be deemed valid by the one offering them, but they are unacceptable to the Master. Do you notice the Master's directive so that his banquet hall will be filled? He sends his servant to: "Go out quickly into the streets and alleys of the town and bring in the poor, the crippled, the blind and the lame. Go out to the roads and country lanes and make them come in, so that my house will be full." In other words, find the "little boats, little people and other sheep." Don't hesitate to include the unattractive and unworthy, the disenfranchised and dysfunctional. The servant is to search for, seek and find the "little boats, little people and the other sheep" and bring them to the Great Banquet.

The words of Jesus that immediately precede this Parable of the Great Banquet are given in Luke 14:12-14 (NIV). They are His guideline for one's attitude and approach to ministry. This may prove to be one of the most glaring places of disobedience within the body of Christ. What does Jesus want His body, the Church, to do in His name? He makes His heart and desire clearly known: "Then Jesus said to his host, when you give a luncheon or dinner, do not invite your friends, your brothers or relatives, or your rich neighbors; if you do, they may invite you back and so you will be repaid. But when you give a banquet, invite the poor, the crippled, the lame, the blind, and you will be blessed. Although they cannot repay you, you will be repaid at the resurrection of the righteous." Could it be that failure to practice this instruction of the Lord Jesus Christ is one of the reasons why the Banquet Halls (the Churches), all across our nation are more empty that filled? It may be that the type of individual Jesus said should be invited to the banquet just doesn't measure up to our personal standards. One can become convinced: "They are not our kind of people." Did Jesus Christ consider anyone as "not My kind of people"? Did Jesus place any restriction regarding who the servant should bring to His Banquet Table? Was anyone off-limits? What about the unlikely or unsavory, should they be invited and brought to the Master's Banquet Table? Should those who frighten us be invited and brought? Should anyone, for any reason, be avoided and remain uninvited? What does the Master want His servants to do and who does He direct should be contacted and brought to His Banquet? Do we attempt to re-write The Master's invitation?

All would do well to remember the words of I Corinthians 1:26-31 (NIV), "Brothers, think of what you were when you were called. Not many of you were wise by human standards; not many were influential; not many were of noble birth. But God chose the foolish things of the world to shame the wise; God chose the weak things of the world to shame the strong. He chose the lowly things of this world and the despised things -- and the things that are not-- to nullify the things that are, so that no one may boast before him. It is because of him that you are in Christ Jesus, who has become for us wisdom from God -- that is, our righteousness, holiness and redemption. Therefore, as it is written: Let him who boasts boast in the Lord."

In some Sermon Notes of Erwin Lutzer, the Pastor of Moody Church in Chicago, Illinois, he jotted the following: "Sometimes it seems God puts His hand on the wrong person. He chooses those who would be considered the least likely to succeed and elevates them to a position of responsibility. The story is told of Queen Victoria of England who used to tell people she was thankful for the letter 'M' in the Bible. When asked what she meant, she would quote First Corinthians chapter one where it says, "You see you're calling brother, not many wise, not many noble, not many foolish are chosen." I'm thankful that he didn't say, "not any noble." I'm thankful for the letter "M." He goes on to comment, "We cannot predict whom God will choose for positions of responsibility. He takes those who are in the shadows and brings them into the light. He takes someone whose family has 'written him off,' and inscribes his name in the Book of Life. The lowly are exalted and the mighty are brought low. He raises the poor from the dust, and lifts the needy from the ash heap, to make them sit with princes, with the princes of His People." He based this thought on the words from Psalm 113:5-9 (NIV), "Who is like the Lord our God, the One who sits enthroned on high, who stoops down to look on the heavens and the earth? He raises the poor from the dust and lifts the needy from the ash heap; he seats them with princes, with the princes of their people. He settles the barren woman in her home as a happy mother of children. Praise the Lord."

Despite the word of the Lord, those who offered their excuses, might now offer criticism and condemnation for bringing "those kind of people" to the Banquet. However, The Master is not governed by their criticism nor their condemnation. He is governed by His will and His purpose. *The Message Paraphrase* renders Luke 14:21-24, "The servant went back and told the master what had happened. He was outraged and told the servant: Quickly, get out into the city streets and alleys. Collect all who look like they need a square meal, all the misfits and homeless and wretched you can lay your hands on, and bring them here. The servant reported back, Master, I did what you commanded and there's still room. The Master said, then go to the country roads. Whoever you find, drag them in. I want my house full! Let me tell you, not one of those originally invited is going to get so much as a bite at my dinner party." What does this suggest the Master wants as the focus of those who identify themselves as His people? Are you one of those who offers excuses or one who goes out in the name of the Master to compel others to come to His Banquet? Is this a challenge that you should evaluate or reevaluate?

Many years ago, an elder in the Church where I served as Pastor and I travelled to Mission, Kansas for a Church Leader Seminar on Evangelism. The Seminar was sponsored by Campus Crusade for Christ and the primary speakers were Bill Bright, the founder of Campus Crusade and Dr. Henry Brandt, a Christian

Psychologist. One part of the seminar was that the participants would be sent out to present the gospel to four family units in Kansas City. In preparation, everyone was given copies of The Four Spiritual Laws and shown how to use it. A flood of questions followed until Dr. Bright said: "If you keep asking questions about how to do evangelism, you'll never fulfill this assignment of going out and doing it." One other surprising, but perceptive statement he made was: "We know that some of you will not do this assigned task. We'll be able to tell when we reassemble if you did or did not evangelize." The perception was that he knew some would make excuses so they would be exempt from going and doing it.

As "excuses" are reevaluated, one should do so with a question that was posed to Jesus, namely, "Who is my neighbor?" The question arises in The Parable of The Good Samaritan when Jesus gave this response in Luke 10:30-37 (NIV), "...Jesus said: A man was going down from Jerusalem to Jericho, when he fell into the hands of robbers. They stripped him of his clothes, beat him and went away, leaving him half dead. A priest happened to be going down the same road, and when he saw the man, he passed by on the other side. So too, a Levite, when he came to the place and saw him, passed by on the other side..." Note at this point, that the Priest and Levite had their reasons for excusing themselves from offering any help or ministry to one of the "little boats, little people or other sheep!" They may have been too busy or had an appointment they were trying to keep. There are no limits or boundaries for the excuses one can and does believe are valid. The text in Luke 10 continues: "But a Samaritan, as he traveled, came where the man was; and when he saw him, he took pity on him. He went to him and bandaged his wounds, pouring on oil and wine. Then he put the man on his own donkey, took him to an inn and took care of him. The next day he took out two silver coins and gave them to the innkeeper. Look after him, he said, and when I return, I will reimburse you for any extra expense you may have.

7. A Serious Challenge

Which of these three do you think was a neighbor to the man who fell into the hands of robbers? The expert in the law replied, "The one who had mercy on him. Jesus told him, Go and do likewise." The Samaritan inconvenienced himself and bore the cost in order to provide care for the stranger in dire straits and with considerable need. He was willing to get his hands dirty as he cleaned the wounds and bandaged the victim who was a stranger. Mercy and compassion governed the Samaritan's behavior and action. In reading this account, one can experience a great amount of conviction and guilt because of the numbers of time we had an opportunity to demonstrate mercy but chose to ignore the stranger. The stranger was one of the "little boats, little people or other sheep" who are so frequently ignored or viewed as being insignificant. Too easily and readily, we might've passed by on the other side and avoided the obvious need.

In reviewing this parable, which one of these persons represents you? Which one would you like to be if the parable was speaking about you? Would you be willing to harbor the "little boats" and be host to the "little people" and care for the "other sheep" who live in nearly every community in this nation? There are reminders in God's Word that give instruction of how one should feel, think and act for our Lord. The first is Proverbs 14:21, 31 (NIV), "He who despises his neighbor sins, but blessed is he who is kind to the needy…He who oppresses the poor shows contempt for their Maker, but whoever is kind to the needy honors God." The second references the behavior of the wicked and oppressor. In Psalm 109:16 (NLT), "For he refused all kindness to others; he persecuted the poor and needy, and he hounded the brokenhearted to death." These words speak of the calloused and indifferent individual who has no qualms about trampling on others and ignoring their needs. Such an attitude would view the "little boats" and sink them; view the "little people" and incarcerate or eliminate them; view the "other sheep" and either butcher them or scatter them. Most would deem this overall approach or philosophy to be treachery and barbarism. We need to ask, what about "The Church" and its attitude and actions toward these same people groups? How can we condemn one and condone the other? This borders on a Darwinian philosophy and approach, namely, the survival of the fittest. The *Free Dictionary* defines the phrase "survival of the fittest" as: "Natural selection conceived of as a struggle for life in which only those organisms best adapted to existing conditions are able to survive and reproduce." Overall, it would prove to be a shortsighted and cruel approach to the "little boats, little people and the other sheep" who are scattered all around us and across the globe.

Just some passing observations and rhetorical questions: Have you ever noticed how the ones who have been marginalized because of a physical malady or handicap are usually ready to do what they can for whoever they can? Have you noticed how one who has been marginalized because of his or her ethnic background (Samaritans not especially liked by others) is sometimes better able to show mercy and compassion to others? Why do you think that is true in many instances? When this occurs, doesn't this represent one from the "little boats, little people and other sheep" classification being better able to empathize and to show mercy to some other "little boat or little person or other sheep"? It brings one back to the heart and passion of James 2:5-9 (NKJV) where he frames the issue of "little boats/little people/other sheep" in this manner: "Listen, my beloved brethren: Has God not chosen the poor of this world to be rich in faith and heirs of the kingdom which He promised to those who love Him? But you have dishonored the poor man. Do not the rich oppress you and drag you into the courts? Do they not blaspheme that noble name by which you are called? If you really fulfill the royal law according to the Scripture, You shall love your neighbor as yourself, you do well; but if you show partiality, you commit sin, and are convicted by the law as transgressors." A significant phrase is, "But you have dishonored the poor man" by ignoring him and his needs.

This thought is not far removed from Jesus Who said in the Olivet Discourse when He was separating the sheep from the goats, Matthew 25:31-46 (NKJV), a portion of which reads, "When the Son of Man comes in His glory, and all the holy angels with Him, then He will sit on the throne of His glory. All the nations will be gathered before Him, and He will separate them one from another, as a shepherd divides his sheep from the goats. And He will set the sheep on His right hand, but the goats on the left. Then the King will say to those on His right hand, Come, you blessed of My Father, inherit the kingdom prepared for you from the foundation of the world: for I was hungry and you gave Me food; I was thirsty and you gave Me drink; I was a stranger and you took Me in; I was naked and you clothed Me; I was sick and you visited Me; I was in prison and you came to Me. Then the righteous will answer Him, saying, Lord, when did we see You hungry and feed You, or thirsty and give You drink? When did we see You a stranger and take You in, or naked and clothe You? Or when did we see You sick, or in prison, and come to You?' And the King will answer and say to them, Assuredly, I say to you, inasmuch as you did it to one of the least of these My brethren, you did it to Me."

Jesus is establishing that He has observed how His followers have treated the "little boats, little people and other sheep!" He is looking at their basic needs for survival and whether or not His followers shared His heart and His passion toward the poor and needy. This is the way He intended His Body to interact with those poor and needy in life they have seen or known. They are to be concerned and show mercy and share with others. One would feel certain that this is what He envisioned when He stated in the Sermon on the Mount, Matthew 6:25, 31-33 (NKJV), "Therefore I say to you, do not worry about your life, what you will eat or what you will drink; nor about your body, what you will put on. Is not life more than food and the body more than clothing? Therefore do not worry, saying, What shall we eat? What shall we drink? What shall we wear? For after all these things the Gentiles seek. For your heavenly Father knows that you need all these things. But seek first the kingdom of God and His righteousness, and all these things shall be added to you." For this to be fully enacted and realized, His followers will have to be responsive and generous. If they see one who is thirsty, give him a beverage; if they see one who is hungry, feed him at your table or give a sufficient amount to quell his hunger; if they see one who is in ragged clothing or naked, provide a garment and clothing to keep such a one warm and protected from the elements. This is God's plan and each of us is to be willing and generous in our response to the needs of others.

There is one more caveat to this instruction of the Master, Jesus Christ. Galatians 6:9-10 (NKJV), "And let us not grow weary while doing good, for in due season we shall reap if we do not lose heart. Therefore, as we have opportunity, let us do good to all, especially to those who are of the household of faith." The "household of faith" should be in focus and with concern. The paraphrase in *The Message* seems apt. "So let's not allow ourselves to get fatigued doing good. At the right time we will harvest a good crop if we don't give up, or quit. Right now, therefore, every time we get the chance, let us work for the benefit of all, starting with the people closest to us in the community of faith." The directives of The Master and these Scriptural instructions bring to mind a dear lady who was a member in a Church where I served as pastor. Everyone who knew and appreciated her referred to her lovingly as "Aunt Stella." She appeared to be a very unlikely person who would be used to touch the lives of the "little boats, little people and other sheep." She was a lady who personified caring for others. She knew those who had particular needs and she was always seeking ways to meet their needs. "Aunt Stella" was known to walk up to a person and ask: "What size shoes are you wearing? How many pairs of shoes do you own? I need a pair for someone who doesn't have any shoes!" The interesting and surprising response was that the person asked would give her a pair of shoes (or anything else that she was looking for to meet the needs of others). Sadly, she became ill and was hospitalized. She was on her deathbed and had the sense that she would not leave the hospital. When my wife and I visited her, she was not focused on her condition but on the needs of others. "Aunt Stella" indicated to my wife the things she had gathered for others, where the items were located and who was to receive them. She died a few days later. I have thought about the numbers of people who were brought to The Master's Banquet Table because of "Aunt Stella's" care and kindness. She saw people with needs and tried to alleviate them. No one was to be avoided or deemed insignificant in the eyes of "Aunt Stella." The culture and world today would be a better place if there were more individuals with Aunt Stella's care, concern and kindness. May her tribe increase!

Some may wonder how effectively the household of faith responds and operates in terms of practical need. In some places, it works well to a point. In other places, it is hindered by a bureaucratic approach and decision-making processes, as well as opinions offered about the one seeking or needing assistance. There are times when a person with need is thought to be a person who is "well off" or "they have their own people" who can help them. While it may be "well-intentioned" and "informative" it nevertheless rationalizes away the need, the person, and the opportunity to act biblically "especially with those who are of the household of faith." It causes undue delays and missed opportunities. It leads us back to James 2:14-18 (NKJV), "What does it profit, my brethren, if someone says he has faith but does not have works? Can faith save him? If a brother or sister is naked and destitute of daily food, and one of you says to them, depart in peace, be warmed and filled, but you do not give them the things which are needed for the body, what does it profit? Thus also faith by itself, if it does not have works, is dead. But someone will say, You have faith, and I have works. Show me your faith without your works, and I will show you my faith by my works." As was stated earlier, the spiritual DNA of the follower of Christ gives evidence of one who is involved in a caring and sharing ministry for those with needs. It involves the extent with which this ministry is done toward all people, but especially to those who are of the household of faith. It shows a profile that this is the normal reflex activity of God's people. When we come before the Lord at the day when sheep and goats are separated, we would then be more than likely to ask the Lord, "When did we do these things?" It is at that point when we will hear the words: "Inasmuch as you did it to one of these "little boats, little people and other sheep," you did it unto Me."

APPLICATION and QUESTIONS:

If a Church has a Deacon's Fund, is that a proxy account that alleviates the responsibility and obligation of the Church Member to be involved in a caring and sharing ministry?

What if the Deacons meet only once a month to consider needs, should the Church Member step in and act in the immediate by assisting the one with need?

In some places, Churches make funds available to the City Hall for distribution to the needy or one requesting some gasoline or a meal. The idea is for there to be a Driver License check and a voucher signed. Is that an adequate response to a needy person? Is that a correct biblical approach?

Based upon one's personal involvement and concerns for the needy, if Jesus Christ came and separated sheep from goats in your Church, who among you would be with the sheep and how many would be with the goats?

On what biblical basis, do you believe you will be numbered with the sheep?

On what works basis, do you believe that you have met God's standard so that you will be numbered with the sheep?

When was the last time you saw someone thirsty, and gave them a drink; or hungry, and gave them food; or with insufficient clothing, and you gave them a garment? If that is the criteria by which one is assessed before the Lord, should it be reviewed and revamped by each of us?

> *And whoever gives one of these little ones only a cup of cold water… he shall by no means lose his reward.*
> Matthew 10:42 (NKJV)

> *By and by when I look on His face, I'll wish I had given Him more.*
> *More, so much more, More of my life than I e'er gave before*
> *By and by when He holds out His hands, I'll wish I had given Him more.*
> Grace Reese Adkins – 1948

8. A Serious Trend

Trends within the culture usually have an influence and impact on the trends in religion. More than eighty years ago, the issue within religion was the conflict between Modernism/Liberalism and Fundamentalism. In an effort to combat this trend, J. Gresham Machen wrote and published a book entitled, *Christianity and Liberalism*. He offered his own reason for writing this tome: "In my little book, *Christianity and Liberalism*, 1923, I tried to show that the issue in the Church of the present day is not between two varieties of the same religion, but, at bottom, between two essentially different types of thought and life. There is much interlocking of the branches, but the two tendencies, Modernism and supernaturalism, or (otherwise designated) non-doctrinal religion and historic Christianity, spring from different roots. In particular, I tried to show that Christianity is not a 'life,' as distinguished from a doctrine, and not a life that has doctrine as its changing symbolic expression, but that exactly the other way around, it is a life founded on a doctrine."

Emerging from the debate between Liberalism and Fundamentalism was a summary statement regarding the Five Fundamentals that should be embraced. The Fundamentals were not to be diminished or compromised by anyone seeking admission as a minister. A man was required to affirm his belief in and adherence to: The inspiration and inerrancy of Scripture; The deity of Jesus Christ; The virgin birth of Christ; The substitutionary, atoning work of Christ on the cross; and The physical resurrection and the personal bodily return of Christ to the earth. Because of this on-going debate, church denominations saw divisions; new foreign mission boards were started; new seminaries were established; and new Churches were begun. The litmus test for those desiring to minister in the more conservative and fundamentalist groups had to embrace, unequivocally, the Five Fundamentals. Other attachments to The Fundamentals were agreed to, such as holding to a premillennial eschatology, and identifying with a declaration on the separation of the believer from worldly practices. An example of this declaration is a statement by the Bible Presbyterian Church in the Harvey Cedars Resolution of 1945: "In conformity to the Word of God, and without adding thereto any rules binding the conscience, we do hereby urge our membership to lead a holy life separated from worldly sin. We hold that the participation in games commonly used for gambling sets a snare for our young people, introducing them to gambling associates and leading them in this evil practice. We hold that the patronage of the commercial theatre is not conducive to the development of the spiritual life. We hold that the promiscuous familiarity between the sexes in modern society in the modern dance and in other modern social customs sets dangerous temptations before the young. We also desire to declare that we deem it wise to pursue the course of total abstinence with regard to alcoholic beverages, and also tobacco; and furthermore we are unalterably opposed to the modern saloon, and the liquor traffic in general. We urge all ministers and Christian leaders among us to discourage these and other worldly practices among the Lord's people, and to give their testimony uncompromisingly against all forms of sin."

These statements and principles served as a type of litmus test for all who desired to be ministers in the Bible Presbyterian Church. Some viewed the matters of personal separation differently, and it became a source of friction and debate over the years. Romans 14 was a reference point in terms of "the weaker brother" and how he was to be considered, defined and treated. In Romans 14:1-5 (NKJV), "Receive one who is weak in the faith, but not to disputes over doubtful things. For one believes he may eat all things, but he who is weak eats only vegetables. Let not him who eats despise him who does not eat, and let not him who does not eat judge him who eats; for God has received him. Who are you to judge another's servant? To his own master he stands or falls. Indeed, he will be made to stand, for God is able to make him stand. One person esteems one day above another; another esteems every day alike. Let each be fully convinced in his own mind."

Romans 14:12-15 (NKJV) continues the thought and consideration one should have for another within the body of Christ. The text states: "So then each of us shall give account of himself to God. Therefore let us not judge one another anymore, but rather resolve this, not to put a stumbling block or a cause to fall in our brother's way. I know and am convinced by the Lord Jesus that there is nothing unclean of itself; but to him who considers anything to be unclean, to him it is unclean. Yet if your brother is grieved because of your food, you are no longer walking in love. Do not destroy with your food the one for whom Christ died."

Even though there was a variation in the exegesis of this Chapter, there were also areas of unanimity, such as, Romans 14:19-23 (NKJV), "Therefore let us pursue the things which make for peace and the things by which one may edify another. Do not destroy the work of God for the sake of food. All things indeed are pure, but it is evil for the man who eats with offense. It is good neither to eat meat nor drink wine nor do anything by which your brother stumbles or is offended or is made weak. Do you have faith? Have it to yourself before God. Happy is he who does not condemn himself in what he approves. But he who doubts is condemned if he eats, because he does not eat from faith; for whatever is not from faith is sin." While the resolution on Christian Liberty matters was not binding, it was handled as though it was written in stone. Of course, a pendulum is known by its swinging movement, and so it is in the Church today. There has been a movement toward laxity in these matters over the years. As a popular advertisement used by a tobacco company in their attempt to gain women smokers was wont to say, "You've come a long way, baby to get where you've got to today..." Ashamedly and regrettably, in many venues, the Church can echo that same approach today.

In more recent times, a chilling term has emerged as a way to define The Church and the trends within religion. It is, "The Post-Christian Era." Charles Gallup, in his book, *The Next American Spirituality*, defines the Post-Christian Era this way: "In the Post-Christian age, the Christian faith is no longer a strong influence in society." Why has this trend occurred and what has been embraced in the place of Christian faith? Someone offered the following observation: "Christians have always been in the minority; however their voices were heard and respected. They made a difference and influenced the culture." Society knew the Christian had values that needed to be heard and not trampled upon. The Church began to be influenced by the culture and gradually lost its voice and influence to the culture. A whole array of "isms" began to be examined, considered and embraced within the Church. A thumbnail sketch of a few of them is: Materialism and a focus on the physical world and things; Hedonism and a focus on the things that stimulate and result in pleasure; Secularism and a focus on the other things in one's contemporary sphere that allowed for religion to become a private and leisure interest; Rationalism and a focus on the idea that truth is discovered by man and the use of his mind; Romanticism and a focus on truth is discovered by man in his heart, intuitively, by feelings; Relativism and a focus on the notion that truth is discovered by man in the use of his will, choices and preferences... There is no absolute truth or error, only shades of grey. What is true for you is not true for me, but we can dialogue while respecting each other's beliefs; Pluralism and a focus on the most desirable qualities, namely, tact and tolerance (Political Correctness is built on this approach); Syncretism and a focus on all religions coming together for a common purpose. The conversation must be about the faith community so we can work together to spread "faith" (whatever that is and has become); Humanism and a focus on the need to encompasses atheists and agnostics with the belief that people can build a society in which the human being, with his needs, is central. Secular humanism emphasizes reason, individual freedom, tolerance and the rejection of supernatural and authoritarian beliefs; and relative morality and a focus on the desire that man has believed and has always justified himself by making comparisons with those worse than himself. Conveniently, such a person does not compare himself with God's standard for faith and practice. Without much searching, an average Christian should be able to discern the increasing presence of these things that are a distraction and dilution of the foundational principles upon which The Church is to be built and maintained.

    If there is to be a transformation within the culture, the individual Christian must face whether or not the Word of God is authoritative for one's life. Is one fully persuaded that it is, "the only infallible rule for faith and practice?" Similarly, there should also be an evaluation, an inventory, of one's life in terms of commitment and submission to the Lord Jesus Christ. One cannot allow for a matter-of-fact attitude or a blasé approach to spiritual growth and a walk with the Lord. In other words, the issue is whether or not one has come to a point of taking a serious God seriously? Is God central in your thoughts and in your daily living? Is this the observable behavior of the one who is a professing Christian? In this shift from foundational principles and core values, those who are seemingly unnoticed are the "little boats, little people and other sheep". It appears there is little concern regarding those who are deemed as either little or lesser. The result is that the "little boats, little people and other sheep" who have gone unnoticed for so long are absent from the Church today. Those who have been ignored no longer have any interest in religion as it is practiced today. One can enter many of the historic churches in different towns and cities, and find that children and young people are few and far between. For whatever reason, it is apparent they arrived at a conclusion that the Church was irrelevant, impractical and directionless for them.

Another aspect for consideration is in terms of how the culture is being impacted with the Gospel by those who assert they believe it and have been converted by it. Can others see the impact the Gospel has had on the one who is endeavoring to share it with another? There is a dividing line, a wall, that is separating faith from practice. There is an unequivocal indication of faith in God but also an observable vacillation when it comes to Practice In Obedience To God. There are many reasons that are offered but a summary of them is: an ignorance of what God requires of His people; an indifference to what God requires of His people; or a fear to implement what God has instructed His people to be and do. If we assume it is a fear to implement, what is one fearful of?

There is an interesting study by *Baptist Press*, August 13, 2012 entitled: "Poll: Churchgoers Struggle In Sharing Their Faith," by Jon D. Wilke. The article states: "When it comes to discipleship, those who regularly attend church struggle with sharing Christ with non-Christians, according to a recent study of church going American Protestants. The study, conducted by LifeWay Research, found that 80 percent of those who attend church one or more times a month believe they have a personal responsibility to share their faith, but 61 percent have not told another person about how to become a Christian in the previous six months. The survey also asked how many times they have personally, invited an unchurched person to attend a church service or some other program at your church? Nearly half (48 percent) of church attendees responded, zero. Thirty-three percent of people say they've personally invited someone one or two times, and 19 percent say they've done so on three or more occasions in the last six months…" Why do people neglect to do what they know they ought to do? Is the wall one has erected between faith and practice become impenetrable?

This type of barrier reminds one of the Berlin Wall. It was the physical division between West Germany and East Germany, and the symbolic boundary between democracy and communism during the Cold War. The Berlin Wall was erected in the dead of night and for 28 years (August 13, 1961 until November 9, 1989) it prevented East Germans from fleeing to the West. The destruction of the wall, which was nearly as instantaneous as its creation, was celebrated around the world. It had been erected to keep people under the control of the communist regime, but in time, it was proven to be a failure. Anyone attempting to escape to the West was shot and killed. When the Wall began to be demolished, it signaled a day of victory and celebration when people could move freely once again. It was a long sought after freedom.

In terms of Christian Commitment, the wall that prevents and limits one's Practice of his or her Faith, must be torn down as well. The reason is very basic. There are "little boats, little people and other sheep" who must be reached and nurtured. If the metaphor, "little boats and little people" is extended to the "other sheep," one will need to understand the teaching and principles of Jesus given in John 10:11,16 (NKJV). Jesus said: "I am the good shepherd. The good shepherd gives His life for the sheep…And other sheep I have which are not of this fold; them also I must bring, and they will hear My voice; and there will be one flock and one shepherd." The "sheep" must follow the Shepherd and be nourished in one's relationship with the Lord. The "other sheep" must first find the Shepherd. In John 10:9 (NKJV) Jesus said, "I am the door. If anyone enters by Me, he will be saved, and will go in and out and find pasture." It is the assigned task for those who are already part of the fold to be concerned for the "other sheep" who must be added to the fold. To refuse to be so engaged, is disobedience. Peter heard these words of Jesus, the Good Shepherd, and they would become an important part of his ministry with the persecuted Church. Peter wrote to the leadership, I Peter 5:1-4 (NASB), "Therefore, I exhort the elders among you, as your fellow elder and witness of the sufferings of Christ, and a partaker also of the glory that is to be revealed, shepherd the flock of God among you, exercising oversight not under compulsion, but voluntarily, according to the will of God; and not for sordid gain, but with eagerness; nor yet as lording it over those allotted to your charge, but proving to be examples to the flock. And when the Chief Shepherd appears, you will receive the unfading crown of glory." Shepherding the flock and seeking the "other sheep" who must be brought into the fold is paramount in Peter's words to a Church that was being scattered due to persecution.

In an email from Focus On The Family, August 6, 2012 the following article by Charles J. Chaput, the Catholic Archbishop of Philadelphia, was published and mailed: "Thriving Pastor, The Recipe for American Renewal." The article states, "This past Sunday the Archbishop gave an extended address on how to build a culture of religious freedom in America. He sees what we see, that little by little our liberties are being eroded by legislators and judges. America needs a special kind of citizenry; a mature, well-informed electorate of persons able to reason clearly and rule themselves prudently. If that's true, and it is, then the greatest danger to American liberty in our day is not religious extremism. It's something very different. It's a culture of narcissism that cocoons us in dumbed-down, bigoted news, vulgarity, distraction, and noise, while methodically excluding God from the human imagination. America is now mission territory. Our own failures helped to make it that way. We need to admit that. Then we need to re-engage the work of discipleship to change it...If we want a culture of religious freedom, we need to begin it here, today, now. We live it by giving ourselves wholeheartedly to God and the Gospel of Jesus Christ by loving God with passion and joy, confidence and courage; and by holding nothing back... Scripture says (ESV), 'Unless the Lord builds the house, those who build it labor in vain' (Psalm 127:1). In the end, God is the builder. We're the living stones."

A further illustration of the depravity within our culture appeared in a news item in the *Cincinnati Enquirer*, August 15, 2012. The headline was: "Man Attacked Because Teens Were Just Bored." The news item stated, "Pat Mahaney was walking home Saturday looking forward to a quiet evening watching sports, when something hit him in the back of the head. The next thing he knew he awoke on his neighbor's front step and the life squad was there. Six teenagers were just bored and were looking for something to do. A police report said when they ambushed Mahaney, he was immediately knocked unconscious. The boys face felony charges of aggravated riot and felonious assault. Mahaney was taken to Mercy Mt. Airy Hospital, where he was treated for four days before being released Tuesday. He suffered so many internal injuries that doctors had to insert a tube down his throat to remove all the blood from his stomach. A tube remained in his right nostril Wednesday and blood continued to seep out of his head. His left eye was heavily blackened. Neighbors and police were stunned at the brutality of the attack but police were struck by how cocky the boys were for their age. They were pretty arrogant in the interview with us. It's appalling. I think it's despicable. This appears to be premeditated and there was no remorse on behalf of any of the assailants. Thirteen year-olds ought to be playing basketball, not running the streets looking for ways to entertain themselves at the expense of somebody."

The above account could be repeated many times over. All across the nation, there is unprovoked violence and crime. Many people, too many, have been shot. Some have died, while others were seriously wounded and all have been traumatized. Those involved in the felonious assault, although teenagers, are still minor children who can be and should be in the category of the "little boats, little people or other sheep!" Somehow along the way, has the Church and the Christian failed in the task of making the Gospel known to those who so obviously were in need of it? The decadence of the culture is directly attributable to the reticence or indifference of the Church and the Christian for neglecting their commission obligation and failing to be engaged in a near-neighbor strategy for evangelism and biblical nurture. Why has there been such wide-spread neglect, failure, reticence and indifference? Has the Church forgotten its cultural mandate and become indifferent to the Culture War that is taking place? Can this be a contributing factor to the climate of our times by the overlooking of the "little lambs" in the Church? Can it be that when they deemed the Church irrelevant and hypocritical for them and that the world was more than eager to acknowledge and accept them? It is sad to contemplate and sadder still if that became the contributing factor in their life-change choice.

From 2001 to 2006 (and revived in 2011), there was a reality show on television called *The Fear Factor*. The publicity blurb for the program stated, "A reality series in which contestants compete by performing extreme physical, mental and gastronomic challenges under the supervision of Hollywood stunt coordinators. If they complete the task, they advance. If fear stops them from completing a stunt or they fail the mission, they are eliminated. The contestant that completes three stunts the most efficiently takes home the grand prize of up to $50,000." Let's single out just two statements: "If they complete the task, they advance..." and "If fear keeps them from completing a stunt or they fail the mission, they are eliminated." There is an obvious application that can and should be made regarding Kingdom work and mission. The assigned task for The Church and individual professing Christian is to Go...Tell (the Gospel)...make disciples. The direction is present for all. The questions: Does one have the will and commitment to accept the responsibility and to press on in order to accomplish the task? Does one have what it takes to endure adversity or difficulty? If so, it means advance. What about the one for whom the challenge seems impossible and too great? They begin the pursuit of the goal but many times, quickly, they begin to draw back and stop. They are unable or unwilling to complete the assigned task. The purpose statement of *The Fear Factor* states, "If fear keeps them from completing a stunt or they fail the mission, they are eliminated." Is that not a deserved result when it comes to the commission duty and how the follower of Christ has accepted his or her responsibility?

What is the purpose and goal of the mission given to the followers of Jesus Christ? In the high priestly prayer of Jesus, John 17:18-23 (NKJV), He prays: "As You sent Me into the world, I also have sent them into the world. And for their sakes I sanctify Myself, that they also may be sanctified by the truth. I do not pray for these alone, but also for those who will believe in Me through their word; that they all may be one, as You, Father, are in Me, and I in You; that they also may be one in Us, that the world may believe that You sent Me. And the glory which You gave Me I have given them, that they may be one just as We are one: I in them, and You in Me; that they may be made perfect in one, and that the world may know that You have sent Me, and have loved them as You have loved Me." Jesus is praying for those "…who will believe in Me through their word…" It is the expectation of Jesus Christ that His followers will make His Word known. His Word is to become our word. His mission is to become our mission. His will is to become our will. When will this truth be embraced and implemented? If not now, when; if not here, where; if not these little boats, people, sheep, then what boats, people and sheep will we care about and minister to in Jesus name?

Reflect back on the statement of *The Fear Factor*. The use of the word "fear" should capture one's attention. Fear is the factor that causes one to "fail" the mission. Fear will paralyze and immobilize one. Fear will short-circuit one's foundational principles and core values, if it can. Fear will cause one to shrink back like a coward rather than marching forward and displaying courage. Fear will bring about failure, namely, failure to go and do the assigned kingdom task. There is a dramatic scene recorded in I Samuel 17:1-11 (NIV). "Now the Philistines gathered their forces for war and…Saul and the Israelites assembled and…drew up their battle line to meet the Philistines. The Philistines occupied one hill and the Israelites another, with the valley between them. A champion named Goliath, who was from Gath, came out of the Philistine camp…Goliath stood and shouted to the ranks of Israel: Why do you come out and line up for battle? Am I not a Philistine, and are you not the servants of Saul? Choose a man and have him come down to me. If he is able to fight and kill me, we will become your subjects; but if I overcome him and kill him, you will become our subjects and serve us. Then the Philistine said: This day I defy the ranks of Israel! Give me a man and let us fight each other. On hearing the Philistine's words, Saul and all the Israelites were dismayed and terrified."

This is a decisive moment, a one-on-one/all or nothing challenge. What does Saul, the King and the Israelites (the army) do when they see and hear Goliath? Verse 11 states, "They were dismayed and terrified." The MSG paraphrase simply states, "When Saul and his troops heard the Philistine's challenge, they were terrified and lost all hope." The NLT renders it, "When Saul and the Israelites heard this, they were terrified and deeply shaken." It was a serious and frightening moment. No one in the entire army of Israel was willing to accept the challenge; or felt equal to that task and risk; or ready to die at the hands of the giant. How different this challenging moment was from that faced by the Apostle Paul in Acts 20. When faced with the risk, danger and the possible loss of his life, the Apostle Paul stated (Acts 20:24, NIV), "However, I consider my life worth nothing to me, if only I may finish the race and complete the task the Lord Jesus has given me, the task of testifying to the gospel of God's grace." The NLT captures the thrust of the verse, "But my life is worth nothing unless I use it for doing the work assigned me by the Lord Jesus, that is, the work of telling others the Good News about God's wonderful kindness and love."

The war situation changes dramatically in I Samuel 17:40-52 (NIV). What new thing has taken place? Who would volunteer to face the giant of the Philistines? Who would risk his life in this impossible and high risk confrontation? David, who was not even in the army of Saul, had volunteered to bring the giant down. He wasn't afraid of him. He had rescued his sheep from bears and lions. They were big, and loud, and fierce, but he prevailed against them, and he is convinced that Goliath will be like one of the wild beasts that he has conquered. The text states, David "...took his staff in his hand, chose five smooth stones from the stream, put them in the pouch of his shepherd's bag and, with his sling in his hand, approached the Philistine. Meanwhile, the Philistine, with his shield bearer in front of him, kept coming closer to David. He looked David over and saw that he was only a boy, ruddy and handsome, and he despised him. He said to David, "Am I a dog, that you come at me with sticks?" And the Philistine cursed David by his gods. "Come here, he said, and I'll give your flesh to the birds of the air and the beasts of the field!" David said to the Philistine, "You come against me with sword and spear and javelin, but I come against you in the name of the Lord Almighty, the God of the armies of Israel, whom you have defied. This day the Lord will hand you over to me, and I'll strike you down and cut off your head. Today I will give the carcasses of the Philistine army to the birds of the air and the beasts of the earth, and the whole world will know that there is a God in Israel. All those gathered here will know that it is not by sword or spear that the Lord saves; for the battle is the Lord's, and he will give all of you into our hands." As the Philistine moved closer to attack him, David ran quickly toward the battle line to meet him. Reaching into his bag and taking out a stone, he slung it and struck the Philistine on the forehead. The stone sank into his forehead, and he fell face down on the ground. So David triumphed over the Philistine with a sling and a stone; without a sword in his hand he struck down the Philistine and killed him. "David ran and stood over him. He took hold of the Philistine's sword and drew it from the scabbard. After he killed him, he cut off his head with the sword. When the Philistines saw that their hero was dead, they turned and ran. Then the men of Israel and Judah surged forward with a shout and pursued the Philistines…"

David demonstrated fearlessness before the enemy and great confidence in the Lord. He didn't walk into the conflict. The text states, "David ran quickly toward the battle line to meet him." David did not do what he did so he would be seen as a hero. The summary of his intent is, "All those gathered here will know that it is not by sword or spear that the Lord saves; for the battle is the Lord's, and he will give all of you into our hands." There's the key for all service being attempted and done, "The battle is the Lord's." What he did was to show: "All those gathered here will know…that the Lord saves…" When you consider reaching out to your near-neighbor, are you doing it in your strength or the strength of the Lord? Do you, like David, run quickly to the battle line to meet the challenge? Are you doing it so you will receive acclaim, or so that all will know that it is the Lord Who saves? We need to grasp the fact and reality that it is all of and for God, and God Alone. There is a meaningful song sung and popularized by Steve Green with that title.

> God and God Alone
> created all these things we call our own
> From the mighty to the small the Glory in them all is
> God's and God's alone.
> God and God alone

reveals the truth of all we call unknown
and the best and worst of man
won't change the Master's plan it's
God's and God's alone.

God and God alone
will be the joy of our eternal home
He will be our one desire
Our hearts will never tire of
God's and God's alone.
Chorus:
God and God alone
is fit to take the universe's throne
Let everything that lives reserve it's truest praise for
God and God alone.

 The lyric is useful as it reminds and enables one to think more completely about God every day and in all aspects of life. It serves one's focus well and the maintenance of a balanced perspective in terms of the world and culture in which one lives and for which one has responsibility. The "little boats, little people and other sheep" are always present with us and must be part of one's ongoing concern. We cannot and should not ignore them or view them as being insignificant, inconsequential or unnecessary.

 In a practical way, the lyric of God and God Alone was an actual part of the daily life of the Psalmist. In Psalm 63:1-3 (NKJV), he wrote, "O God, You are my God; early will I seek You; my soul thirsts for You; my flesh longs for You In a dry and thirsty land Where there is no water. So I have looked for You in the sanctuary, to see Your power and Your glory. Because Your loving-kindness is better than life, My lips shall praise You." It was similar for the prophet Isaiah. In Isaiah 26:3-4, 9 (NLT), we read, "You will keep in perfect peace all who trust in you, whose thoughts are fixed on you! Trust in the Lord always, for the Lord God is the eternal Rock... With my soul I have desired You in the night, Yes, by my spirit within me I will seek You early..." Both writers share that it is an internal longing after God as one begins each new day with Him.

There is a very meaningful pair of Psalms written at a time when David was concerned for his life. In Psalm 3:5-6 (NKJV), he wrote: "I lay down and slept; I woke again, for the Lord sustained me. I will not be afraid of many thousands of people who have set themselves against me all around." In the companion passage, Psalm 4:7-8 (NKJV), David writes: "You have put more joy in my heart...In peace I will both lie down and sleep; for you alone, O Lord, make me dwell in safety." It represents a quiet spirit at all times because one is resting in the Lord and casting all of one's care upon Him. Is this your prayer and experience as you begin each new day with the Lord? As you conclude your day, is He still present in your thoughts?

APPLICATION and QUESTIONS:

Do you think it matters whether or not you become engaged in evangelism and outreach ministry? Is it practical and relevant for our day?

Are you more influenced by our culture rather than being an influence to and in the culture? Why?

What one thing impacts your "fear factor" in terms of what you are willing and ready to do in the Lord's strength?

When an opportunity to minister to another is obviously yours, do you run to meet that challenge or do you procrastinate and inordinately delay following-through?

Have you done anything to prepare yourself so you can address needs within our culture? What have you done? Have you read books; been to a contemporary Bible Study; attended a seminar?

In your opinion, what are the most pressing trends and issues in our culture that should be addressed? Why?

In what way(s) should the pressing trends and issues of our day be addressed?

In what you do, are the "little boats, little people and other sheep" part of your concern and within your vision? In what way?

Do you know the reality of a quiet spirit as you rest in the Lord, and as you cast all of your care upon Him?

Peace, perfect peace, in this dark world of sin?
The blood of Jesus whispers peace within.

Peace, perfect peace, by thronging duties pressed?
To do the will of Jesus, this is rest.
Edward H. Bickersteth, Jr.

9. A Serious Drift

Hebrews 2:1-3 (NIV) contains the following admonition, "We must pay more careful attention, therefore, to what we have heard, so that we do not drift away. For if the message spoken by angels was binding, and every violation and disobedience received its just punishment, how shall we escape if we ignore such a great salvation? This salvation, which was first announced by the Lord, was confirmed to us by those who heard him." Two of the key components for our consideration are the need to pay more careful attention, and the inherent danger in drifting. The basic application is to pay more careful attention to what has been declared in Hebrews 1 about Jesus Christ. The next application is the command in Hebrews 2 to guard against drifting away from the great salvation in Jesus Christ. Why is this an important instruction and command? In matters of faith and practice, there is a very clear distinction between what is right and wrong. Within interpersonal relationships, there is a correct and normal behavior versus an incorrect and abnormal behavior. In one's life, if the mind, emotion, and will gravitates or drifts toward malfunction, dysfunction or the abnormal, then there needs to be an assessment and understanding in terms of why this behavior is actuated. What incites an individual to a certain action? What impels and motivates one? Why does the abnormal process begin? Can malfunction, dysfunction and abnormal behaviors be the root of why there is the lack of concern for the "little boats, little people and other sheep"?

In these considerations, we have before us the words of II Timothy 1:7 (ESV), "God gave us a spirit not of fear but of power and love and self-control." In the NIV, "God did not give us a spirit of timidity, but a spirit of power, of love and of self-discipline." In the NKJV, "God has not given us a spirit of fear, but of power and of love and of a sound mind." In these translations, we are given the variants in terms of behavioral foundations that one is to possess and develop, namely, self-control, self-discipline and a sound mind. I am grateful for the dear soul with whom I visited shortly before her death. I asked her what promise or instruction in God's Word had been important to her over the years of her lifetime. Without hesitancy, she quoted II Timothy 1:7 (KJV) and when she reached the last phrase of the verse, she raised her hand and placed a finger on her temple and said: "a sound mind...sound mind." At her funeral, I was honored to be able to share her testimony with those who had gathered. The other expressed concern for her was that the next generation and their children would have that same commitment. She would concur that the goal of every biblical Christian should be the possession of "a sound mind...self-control...self-discipline." This is part of the normal Christian life and one's spiritual DNA.

A parallel passage is Titus 2:1-6 (NKJV). It speaks in an encompassing way of how the entire household of believers is to behave "normally" before each other: "But as for you, speak the things which are proper for sound doctrine: that the older men be sober, reverent, temperate, sound in faith, in love, in patience; the older women likewise, that they be reverent in behavior, not slanderers, not given to much wine, teachers of good things, that they admonish the young women to love their husbands, to love their children, to be discreet, chaste, homemakers, good, obedient to their own husbands, that the word of God may not be blasphemed. Likewise exhort the young men to be sober-minded..." The word translated sober and sound is parallel to the sound mind reference to Timothy. Paul is indicating that there is a normal godly lifestyle that can be maintained in any culture and in any period of history. The goal is to remind everyone regarding how they are to live. The secularist will doubtlessly see it as "abnormal" but our commitment is to model it as the "normal" for a world and culture in a state of flux. A major issue in the twenty-first century is that the secular has been allowed to have a considerable influence within the Church. As a result, there has been a drifting away within the Church from foundational truths and core values. The pattern has been obvious for some time. Whether it is blatant liberalism, or psychological emphases (Positive Thinking), or materialism (Prosperity Gospel), or Liberation Theology (Social Gospel), they all ultimately accelerate the drifting away from the great salvation in Jesus Christ alone. The water becomes muddy and people become misled into a belief that it is Jesus plus something else. It should not be surprising that there is considerable confusion when it comes to determining that which is normal versus that which is abnormal.

There is another factor that contributes to the drift away from the sure foundation and core values of the Church and in the lives of those who are seeking for that which is "normal." The Lord calls on his prophet to deliver a message to the people and to address their abnormal behavior. Part of that message is stated in Jeremiah 5:21-31 (NIV Selected), "Hear this, you foolish and senseless people, who have eyes but do not see, who have ears but do not hear: Should you not fear me declares the Lord? Should you not tremble in my presence…But these people have stubborn and rebellious hearts; they have turned aside and gone away. They do not say to themselves, Let us fear the Lord our God…your sins have deprived you of good. Among my people are wicked men…their houses are full of deceit; they have become rich and powerful….Their evil deeds have no limit, they do not plead the case of the fatherless to win it, they do not defend the rights of the poor. Should I not punish them for this, declares the Lord? Should I not avenge myself on such a nation as this? A horrible and shocking thing has happened in the land: The prophets prophesy lies, the priests rule by their own authority, and my people love it this way. But what will you do in the end?" The central point that applies to their plight in Jeremiah's day has application in our day, namely, "The prophets prophesy lies, the priests rule by their own authority, and my people love it this way."

As an alternative to The Lord and His Word, people turn to other and lesser things for answers and direction for their lives. They sense something is not as normal as they would like it to be. In their quest, they resort to other avenues and areas. Among them are psychology, philosophy and sociology. While it is easy to access materials on the subject of abnormal behavior, if there is to be an assessment, analysis and diagnosis about abnormal behavior, what standard is to be used as a frame of reference regarding normal behavior? To what is it being compared? Very simply, what is normal behavior? One should have an idea and concept of normal before assessing and declaring what is abnormal. There should be a value and standard by which normal and abnormal can be measured. There also has to be an understanding in terms of man and what makes him different from all other creatures. For the secularist, their standard is psychology, philosophy and sociology. For the spiritual-minded, their standard is God's Word. Therein is the conflict between the two, namely, the soul of man is eternal. How does one address the soul of man? What source can determine the differentiation between the normal and abnormal? Can the secular man explain to a spiritual man the distinction between that which is normal and that which is abnormal and applicable to one's soul?

The contributors to Wikipedia write of normal behavior in this manner: "Normality…is the state of being normal. Behavior can be normal for an individual…when it is consistent with the most common behavior for that person. Normal is also used to describe when someone's behavior conforms to the most common behavior in society…Definitions of normality vary by person, time, place, and situation – it changes along with changing societal standards and norms…Although it is difficult to define normality, since it is a flexible concept, the existence of these ramifications also makes it an important definition. The most comprehensive attempt to distinguish normality from abnormality comes from clinical psychology, in the *Diagnostics and Statistics Manual*. The DSM shows how normality is dependent on situation, how it changes throughout history and how it often involves value judgments."

Did you note the areas for discussion and determination of "What Is Normal?" The suggestion made: "What is normal is discussed in many fields, including philosophy, psychology and sociology…" One of the key issues with these areas is that the defining of what is normal becomes a subjective process that is absent from any true measure or standard by which the theory and hypothesis can be compared. It would seem that a requirement for an objective standard for what is normal would be a minimum requirement for this study. For it to be a comprehensive and complete study, it should include the spiritual, that is, the soul-spirit and what relationship that area of development or neglect the spiritual impacts. What is normal or abnormal regarding the soul and spirit of man? Absent that, the conclusions would be more theory than reality and slanted in such a manner that it could result in considerable harm being done rather than a therapeutic result being accomplished. Man needs to be understood in the totality of the creation and how he was fearfully and wonderfully made, as well as knowing the reality of who he is, namely, one who has been created in the image of God.

The Mayo Clinic Staff, on the question of: Mental Health: What's Normal, What's Not? concluded: "Why is it so tough to tell what's normal? It's often difficult to distinguish normal mental health from mental illness because there's no easy test to show if something's wrong. Mental health conditions are diagnosed and treated based on signs and symptoms, as well as on how much the condition affects your daily life. Signs and symptoms can affect your: (1) Behavior. Obsessive hand-washing or drinking too much alcohol might be signs of a mental health condition; (2) Feelings.

Sometimes a mental health condition is characterized by a deep or ongoing sadness, euphoria or anger; (3) Thinking. Delusions such as thinking that the television is controlling your mind or thoughts of suicide might be symptoms of a mental health condition..." The secularists try to figure out human behavior based upon physical and psychological factors. When they do so, they omit or neglect how man was created and what man is. He is created with a body, soul and spirit and he possesses a mind, emotions and a will that enable him to know, think and act. He is made wonderfully well, albeit he is a complex person that is impacted by the nurturing of the body, soul and spirit as well as the development and maturation of the mind (think), emotion (feel), and will (do). As one thinks objectively and remembers that God is the Creator, it is appropriate to remind ourselves of how man was created in a very special way, in the image of God.

The words in Psalm 139:13-18 (NKJV) encapsulate The Creator's design of man: "For you formed my inward parts; you knitted me together in my mother's womb. I praise you, for I am fearfully and wonderfully made. Wonderful are your works; my soul knows it very well. My frame was not hidden from you, when I was being made in secret, intricately woven in the depths of the earth. Your eyes saw my unformed substance; in your book were written, every one of them, the days that were formed for me, when as yet there was none of them. How precious to me are your thoughts, O God! How vast is the sum of them! If I would count them, they are more than the sand. I awake, and I am still with you." If only there was a way to have the secularist consider this process of The Creator when they pursue their study in terms of, what is normal. It is not surprising to find that so many are adrift and heading toward uncertain, perilous waters. In the studies done by various professionals and groups, one study has five categories into which they can identify the abnormal man. The last of those categories is the social-cultural. It concludes that abnormal behavior is learned within a social context ranging from the family, to the community, to the culture. This is how the secularist views and analyzes man and that which determines who/what is normal versus who/what is abnormal. The larger question should be focused on man in the image of God and whether or not he should be content with that which is merely normal. In terms of how he was made and what he should be, should man be seen and understood as being just normal? Should man not be in pursuit of that which is above normal? To remain normal, man would just drift along, floating in and out of abnormal to normal. This kind of drift is fraught with danger.

What is the standard by which man created in the image of God will be measured? Deep within man is a longing in his heart and soul. That longing flows from how he has been made and structured. We learn from Ecclesiastes 3:10-14 (NIV), "I have seen the burden God has laid on men. He has made everything beautiful in its time. He has also set eternity in the hearts of men; yet they cannot fathom what God has done from beginning to end…I know that everything God does will endure forever; nothing can be added to it and nothing taken from it. God does it so that men will revere him." The fact of "eternity in the hearts of men" is that which tugs within one to find the source that can satisfy that longing and fill that heart. A hymn written in the eighth century encapsulates the longing and desire deep within the soul of one who wants to be above normal in the ongoing relationship with the Lord Jesus Christ. Man's aspiration and desire is found in the words of the traditional Irish Hymn, "Be Thou My Vision" (Words attributed to Dallán Forgaill, the sixth century Irish poet):

> Be Thou my Vision, O Lord of my heart;
> Naught be all else to me, save that Thou art.
> Thou my best Thought, by day or by night,
> Waking or sleeping, Thy presence my light.

9. A Serious Drift

> Be Thou my Wisdom, and Thou my true Word;
> I ever with Thee and Thou with me, Lord;
> Thou my great Father, I Thy true son;
> Thou in me dwelling, and I with Thee one.

Let us suppose that the secularist would be willing to entertain the Spiritual composition of created man and what is basic for him to be in the image of God. Where would one begin? We will start with a passage that states what the Lord requires, namely, "With what shall I come before the Lord and bow down before the exalted God? Shall I come before him with burnt offerings, with calves a year old? Will the Lord be pleased with thousands of rams, with ten thousand rivers of oil? Shall I offer my first-born for my transgression, the fruit of my body for the sin of my soul? He has showed you, O man, what is good. And what does the Lord require of you? To act justly and to love mercy and to walk humbly with your God" (Micah 6:6-8, NIV). The question and answer is in Micah 6:8: "What does the Lord require?" The answer is succinct. The Lord requires for one "to act justly and to love mercy and to walk humbly with your God."

When a study is done regarding malfunction, it does so because something is not operating or functioning as it should. It represents failure, the imperfect and the irregular. As it pertains to the family, it is a "…failure to show characteristics or fulfilling the purposes accepted as normal or beneficial…" There are books, studies and papers that touch on the subject of: Perspectives on abnormal behavior. A focus and determination reached by those doing such studies includes the following: "Those in the field of abnormal psychology study people's emotional, cognitive, and behavioral problems. Abnormal behavior may be defined as behavior that is disturbing (socially unacceptable), distressing, maladaptive (or self-defeating), and often the result of distorted thoughts (cognitions). Several perspectives (models, approaches derived from data) and theories attempt to explain the causes of abnormal behavior." The secular study is done with a focus limited to a physical-mental perspective in five categories and areas: The medical, the psychodynamic, the behavioral, the cognitive, and the social-cultural. The medical concludes that biological and physiological factors are causes of abnormal behavior. The psychodynamic evolved from Freudian psychoanalytic theory, which contends that psychological disorders are the consequence of anxiety produced by unresolved, unconscious conflicts. The behavioral concludes that abnormal behavior results from faulty or ineffective learning and conditioning. The cognitive concludes that particular thoughts and behaviors are often based upon their false assumptions.

The above normal Christian and godly life is urged in Scripture and is possible. Jesus was very detailed with His followers on how they are to live and act. In the passage that precedes the parable of The Good Samaritan, Jesus was asked a question. He answered it in Luke 10:25-28 (NIV), "On one occasion an expert in the law stood up to test Jesus. Teacher, he asked, what must I do to inherit eternal life? What is written in the Law? He replied. How do you read it? He answered: Love the Lord your God with all your heart and with all your soul and with all your strength and with all your mind; and, Love your neighbor as yourself. You have answered correctly, Jesus replied. Do this and you will live." A. T. Robertson in his *Word Pictures of the New Testament* indicates that Luke 10:27 means, "God is to be loved with all of man's four powers, his heart, soul, strength and mind." It is a total and complete commitment to Him Who loved us and gave Himself for us. It can never be either half-hearted or occasional. In effect, Jesus is saying, count the cost of following Me. It is all or nothing. Jesus does not want, nor will He allow, second-place in your life. Charles A. Tindley wrote a very compelling hymn, "Nothing Between." His Lyric indicates the things that could detour one's level of personal commitment. The song of the heart must be:

> Nothing between my soul and my Savior,
> Naught of this world's delusive dream;
> I have renounced all sinful pleasure;
> Jesus is mine, there's nothing between.
>
> Nothing between, like worldly pleasure;
> Habits of life, though harmless they seem,
> Must not my heart from Him ever sever;
> He is my all, there's nothing between.
>
> Nothing between, like pride or station;
> Self or friends shall not intervene;
> Though it may cost me much tribulation,
> I am resolved, there's nothing between.
>
> Nothing between, even many hard trials,
> Though the whole world against me convene;
> Watching with prayer and much self-denial,
> I'll triumph at last, there's nothing between.
>
> Refrain:
> Nothing between my soul and my Savior,
> So that His blessed face may be seen;
> Nothing preventing the least of His favor;
> Keep the way clear! Let nothing between.

This "Nothing Between" and "Above Normal" life has a very narrow focus. There are characteristics and qualities that cannot and should not be compromised. Two references from God's Word afford us a glimpse into this unique relationship and life commitment. We glean these characteristics and qualities in Colossians 3:5-10 (NIV), "Put to death, therefore, whatever belongs to your earthly nature: sexual immorality, impurity, lust, evil desires and greed, which is idolatry. Because of these, the wrath of God is coming. You used to walk in these ways, in the life you once lived. But now you must rid yourselves of all such things as these: anger, rage, malice, slander, and filthy language from your lips. Do not lie to each other, since you have taken off your old self with its practices and have put on the new self, which is being renewed in knowledge in the image of its Creator." This is how the above normal life is to be lived. It is a standard that should not be ignored or avoided. It should not be entertained with complacency or procrastination. The image of God factor being renewed is knowledge. The goal and commitment is to "put on the new self, which is being renewed in knowledge in the image of its Creator." One would be served well by doing a word study of those things which are to be "put off" as well as those things that are to be "put on".

This same discussion regarding the above normal life and lifestyle is given in Ephesians 4:20-32 (NIV), "You…did not come to know Christ that way. Surely you heard of him and were taught in him in accordance with the truth that is in Jesus. You were taught, with regard to your former way of life, to put off your old self, which is being corrupted by its deceitful desires; to be made new in the attitude of your minds; and to put on the new self, created to be like God in true righteousness and holiness. Therefore each of you must put off falsehood and speak truthfully to his neighbor, for we are all members of one body. In your anger do not sin: Do not let the sun go down while you are still angry, and do not give the devil a foothold. He who has been stealing must steal no longer, but must work, doing something useful with his own hands, that he may have something to share with those in need. Do not let any unwholesome talk come out of your mouths, but only what is helpful for building others up according to their needs, that it may benefit those who listen. And do not grieve the Holy Spirit of God, with whom you were sealed for the day of redemption. Get rid of all bitterness, rage and anger, brawling and slander, along with every form of malice. Be kind and compassionate to one another, forgiving each other, just as in Christ God forgave you." The Image of the God Factor being renewed is in "being created to be like God in true righteousness and holiness." This is the pathway for the one longing for and committed to the above normal life in Christ. Is it your aspiration and goal? Is it a pursuit in which you are realizing progress?

Three aspects of being renewed in the image of God have been stated in Colossians 3 and Ephesians 4. They are knowledge, true righteousness and true holiness. For these three aspects and the other areas indicated, there will be continued honing and refining of the Christian and the disciple who is following and serving Jesus Christ. The normal Christian life is one that is under-construction. It is an ongoing process of growth and development. The following is a reminder of the things one needs to remember and to which one must respond affirmatively. First, Romans 12:1-2 (MSG), "So here's what I want you to do, God helping you: Take your everyday, ordinary life - your sleeping, eating, going-to-work, and walking-around life - and place it before God as an offering. Embracing what God does for you is the best thing you can do for him. Don't become so well-adjusted to your culture that you fit into it without even thinking. Instead, fix your attention on God. You'll be changed from the inside out. Readily recognize what he wants from you, and quickly respond to it. Unlike the culture around you, always dragging you down to its level of immaturity, God brings the best out of you, develops well-formed maturity in you." Paul gives this sound counsel as the basis and means for arriving at the above normal life. Second, I John 2:15-17 (NLT), "Stop loving this evil world and all that it offers you, for when you love the world, you show that you do not have the love of the Father in you. For the world offers only the lust for physical pleasure, the lust for everything we see, and pride in our possessions. These are not from the Father. They are from this evil world. And this world is fading away, along with everything it craves. But if you do the will of God, you will live forever." The very things that would distract and detract one are part and parcel of abnormal behavior. The abnormal behavior is a contributing factor to one's avoidance and treatment of the "little boats, little people and other sheep." Abnormal behavior sees them as inconsequential and insignificant. The commands and conditions of God's Word are the standard and platform where the one seeking above normal behavior can and will stand. It is by those with above normal behavior that the "little boats, little people and other sheep" will be properly regarded as they become recipients of genuine care and recognition as being significant in God's kingdom strategy. Without such care and concern, the "little boats, little people and other sheep" are at risk and in danger of drifting into perilous waters and possible demise.

APPLICATIONS and QUESTIONS:

In a real place and real time, have you ever been in a situation where you were drifting and were incapable to prevent the direction in which you were heading?

If you were drifting, what is the first thing you should do? If you were aware of someone else drifting and imperiled, what should you do?

When "little boats, little people or other sheep" are at risk, what steps would you take to spare them of the pending negative result?

9. A Serious Drift

Be introspective for a moment. Overall, is your life represented by Abnormal Behavior or Above Normal Behavior? Does it matter to you which one it is?

What is the consequence for the one who is indifferent to the foundation and core values that are central to the Above Normal life and lifestyle?

Will the person who is Below Normal gain entrance into the Kingdom of Heaven?

What does Jesus allow and say about the previous question in Matthew 7:21-23? Based upon this passage, what is the singular way and means for being sure of gaining entrance into God's heaven? What does that include?

Do you think the Lord makes any exception to His standard for admission to His heaven? Did he ever make an exception? Did he ever cut anyone some slack?

Do you think your life and lifestyle has any bearing upon the "little boats, little people and other sheep"? In what way?

I will serve thee because I love thee.
I was nothing before you found me.
Heartaches, broken pieces, ruined lives
Are why you died on Calvary.
You have given life to me.
William and Gloria Gaither

10. A Serious Defining Moment

Earlier in this writing, the reference to the "little boats" was said to be a metaphor that would include "little people" and "other sheep." If this was an exegesis on the text, Mark 4:35-41 (NKJV), we would examine the words and phrases within this parable. For instance, let us examine "the other little boats." We would ask: "Why were they there? Who was on board of those little boats? What did they want? What were they seeking?" The text doesn't share those details with us. Perhaps they were there out of curiosity, having seen some miracles and hearing the words of Jesus, and they did not want to miss what he did or said next? Maybe they were there because they wanted to be a part of that special group that was onboard the bigger ship with Jesus! Maybe Jesus would take notice of their diligence and call them to be part of His inner circle of disciples! There are some people who like to be a name-dropper and claim a vicarious association with people of notoriety. With the other little boats, we don't know their reason. All we know is that they were there and caught in the midst of the sudden storm that arose.

There's a webpage titled: "Feed My Sheep" (http://www.feedmysheep.co.uk) that advances an idea or two regarding the little boats. The writer-contributor shares these thoughts and comments on Mark 4:36: "But in his account of the event Mark tells us something Matthew and Luke do not. Now that doesn't mean at all that there's a contradiction between, or an error in the Scriptures. But in his account Mark simply says, 'There were with him other little boats' (Mark 4:36). Up to this point, and as far as most of us are concerned, and even Matthew and Luke for that matter, we're all focused on that one ship where Jesus and His disciples were onboard. But Mark indicates there were other little boats out there, too. Of course there would be. We often get so preoccupied with what's going on in our boat that we hardly recognize that there are other little boats in the sea of life, until someone like Mark comes along to remind us. We think it's really nobody's business what we do over here in our little boat! But there really are other little boats out there in the sea, and what we do over here in our ship, does have an effect on the lives of the people in all those other boats, too, either for good or for bad. The other boats did not know why the storm was stopped. I wonder what the men in those other little boats must have been thinking? Here they are in their boats being tossed to and fro with the winds and the waves. Their boats were filling with water. They were in grave danger of losing their boats, and perhaps drowning! Then suddenly and for no apparent reason at all, the winds hushed and the waves lay quietly in the sea. They, too, were saved by the Master of the sea!"

If we extend our metaphor of "little boats" to the "little people" and "other sheep," we can inquire regarding who they are and if they have special and remedial needs. One possibility regarding who they are may be those identified in an appeal letter sent by World Vision in August 2012. The letter indicated that, "Minute by minute, second by second someone loses the most precious thing in their life - they lose a child, because of hunger. These families need immediate help. For mothers like Magfoula in Mauritania, West Africa, food is either unavailable or unaffordable. As a result, her 15-month-old is barely bigger than a newborn. She says, 'When our rice is finished, my first and only child will die.' He is small, frail, and severely malnourished and desperately needs emergency nutrition and medical care to survive. Millions of boys and girls are facing severe malnourishment and thousands are dying because of hunger every single day."

If you want to know who some of the "the little boats, little people and other sheep" may be, focus on Haiti, the poorest nation in our hemisphere. Think of the storms they have endured on their portion of the island of Hispaniola (the Dominican Republic shares this island). In January 2010, Haiti endured a devastating earthquake, with rain and flooding and mudslides. They have so little and yet they lost what little they had. Relief and aid groups supplied tents for multitudes of people but they are not sufficient to shelter them from the hurricanes that come frequently. As a matter of fact, the organization, Save The Children (http://wwwsavethechildren.org) stated: "Almost 400,000 people still living in tents more than two years after Haiti's devastating earthquake are bracing themselves for the landfall of another huge tropical storm. The Tropical Storm Isaac was forecast to hit Haiti late on Friday, August 24th, 2012, by which time its winds could have strengthened to hurricane force. The storm was expected to bring heavy rain, flash floods and mudslides, posing a serious threat to thousands of families previously made homeless by the enormous earthquake which also destroyed many buildings in the capital, Port-au-Prince. At risk will be the thousands who live in hastily constructed slums in the city. As Isaac bears down on Haiti, thousands of families are relying on flimsy canvas to protect them from a potential hurricane. Hurricanes can cause enormous destruction and even those in permanent buildings are not safe. It's important that we are as ready as possible to reduce risks and to respond to disasters. Families living in Haiti's tent cities are in an extremely precarious situation. They have no-where to go to seek shelter from the storm."

These "little people" groups and individuals dot our globe and nation. They are everywhere. They live in our states, cities, towns, countryside, and neighborhoods. They are people who are there. We know about their existence and some of their need but we can be so focused on "us" and "me" or "I" that we miss seeing or caring for "them" or "they" or the "other unknowns." As my wife and I were driving to a nearby city, we passed a man who was pushing a bicycle through some tall and thick grass on the shoulder of the road. He looked so weary and helpless. We could have stopped and put his bicycle in the back of our truck and gotten him to a place where he could more easily ride it, but we were focused on an appointment that had to be kept and drove on by him. This is similar to another situation. While I was supplying a church approximately 100 miles from our home, every Lord's Day we would drive by a group of four or five men in a very tiny town. They were sitting on a concrete block. They were just there. Every week, we passed them, and one week I shared with the church congregation that I wondered who these men were and why were they sitting there every week. Did they have special needs? Did they know Jesus Christ as their Savior and Lord? Did anyone show any interest in them in any way? Did anyone care? Had anyone ever stopped and tried to find out about these men and their small community? While there was interest in what was being shared, the church was close to 30 miles away. We had occasion to drive through that small community more recently and observed that the concrete block remained but no men were present. We could only wonder where they were or if they were still alive. Those mentioned above represent a small fraction of the "little boats, little people and other sheep" who are here, everywhere, and seemingly unnoticed. They dot our landscape. Some people who look rough, tough and scary will brighten in their countenance when someone takes time to speak kindly with them. It boils down to a risk and reward opportunity. The risk is that some will reject your effort. The reward is that some will be grateful for your friendliness and kindness.

The above descriptions remind us of the third part of the "little boat" metaphor, namely, the "other sheep." We have clear biblical guidance from Jesus Christ regarding the needed focus on the "other sheep." In His discourse on The Good Shepherd, Jesus stated (John 10:16, NIV), "I have other sheep that are not of this sheep pen. I must bring them also. They too will listen to my voice, and there shall be one flock and one shepherd." Jesus prayed (John 17:20-21, NIV), "My prayer is not for them (His disciples) alone. I pray also for those who will believe in me through their message, that all of them may be one, Father, just as you are in me and I am in you. May they also be in us so that the world may believe that you have sent me." The "other sheep" are those who will be brought to Jesus Christ through the faithful declaring of The Gospel.

There is a unique aspect to The Confession and Reinstatement of Peter in John 21:15-17 (NIV), "When they had finished eating, Jesus said to Simon Peter, Simon son of John, do you truly love me more than these? Yes, Lord, he said, you know that I love you. Jesus said, Feed my lambs. Again Jesus said, Simon son of John, do you truly love me? He answered, Yes, Lord, you know that I love you. Jesus said, Take care of my sheep. The third time he said to him, Simon son of John, do you love me? Peter was hurt because Jesus asked him the third time, Do you love me? He said, Lord, you know all things; you know that I love you. Jesus said, feed my sheep." Jesus is not only reinstating Peter into functional ministry, He is also focusing him on the Lambs and Sheep that must be reached and brought into the fold where they can be cared for and nourished. Peter did not fully realize or anticipate who the "other sheep" and "other lambs" would be. Not yet, but very soon he would.

After the ascension of Jesus Christ, and after the Day of Pentecost, and after the ministry is well underway in Acts 1 through 9, Peter will now learn more about what Jesus had in mind when he directed him to care for the lambs and sheep. In Acts 10, a new dimension of ministry will soon confront Peter. Is he ready to accept it and meet this challenge? Will he willingly step out of his safety zone and explore a new horizon of ministry? Will he remember the confession he made before Jesus Christ about loving Him? Will he remember that Jesus Christ told him about Lambs and Sheep that he would have to care for and nourish? Will Peter venture out into something new, regardless of the risk it might entail? Acts 10:1-5 (NKJV) gives us this account, "At Caesarea there was a man named Cornelius, a centurion in what was known as the Italian Regiment. He and all his family were devout and God-fearing; he gave generously to those in need and prayed to God regularly. One day at about three in the afternoon he had a vision. He distinctly saw an angel of God, who came to him and said, Cornelius! Cornelius stared at him in fear. What is it, Lord? he asked. The angel answered, your prayers and gifts to the poor have come up as a memorial offering before God. Now send men to Joppa to bring back a man named Simon who is called Peter."

Meanwhile, in Acts 10:11-20 (NKJV), Peter is having a vision as well. "He saw heaven opened and something like a large sheet being let down to earth by its four corners. It contained all kinds of four-footed animals, as well as reptiles of the earth and birds of the air. Then a voice told him, get up, Peter. Kill and eat. Surely not, Lord! Peter replied. I have never eaten anything impure or unclean. The voice spoke to him a second time, Do not call anything impure that God has made clean. This happened three times, and immediately the sheet was taken back to heaven. While Peter was wondering about the meaning of the vision, the men sent by Cornelius found out where Simon's house was and stopped at the gate. They called out, asking if Simon who was known as Peter was staying there. While Peter was still thinking about the vision, the Spirit said to him, Simon, three men are looking for you. So get up and go downstairs. Do not hesitate to go with them, for I have sent them." What does the vision of all kinds of animals have to do with the men sent by Cornelius who were at his gate? What did unclean animals have to do with people who wanted to see him and take him with them? Did Peter fully appreciate that this was preparation for a new phase of ministry for him? How would he personally handle this cultural transition in his life and ministry?

Acts 10:27-33 (NIV), records that there is a transparent moment between Peter and Cornelius. The text states, "Talking with him, Peter went inside and found a large gathering of people.

He said to them: You are well aware that it is against our law for a Jew to associate with a Gentile or visit him. But God has shown me that I should not call any man impure or unclean. So when I was sent for, I came without raising any objection. May I ask why you sent for me? Cornelius answered: Four days ago I was in my house praying at this hour, at three in the afternoon. Suddenly a man in shining clothes stood before me and said, Cornelius, God has heard your prayer and remembered your gifts to the poor. Send to Joppa for Simon who is called Peter. He is a guest in the home of Simon the tanner, who lives by the sea. So I sent for you immediately, and it was good of you to come. Now we are all here in the presence of God to listen to everything the Lord has commanded you to tell us." A group of people ready to hear, eager to learn, wanting to embrace the Gospel of Jesus Christ had gathered. Peter and his companions would never have imagined that the Gospel and Gentiles would be meshed together. Peter thought in terms of Jewish traditions and cultural boundaries. Apart from the vision and men being sent to bring him to Cornelius, one could easily conclude that Peter never would have gone voluntarily to reach any of the "other sheep." For Peter, the "other sheep" were the Gentiles. Peter summarizes the issue when he said to Cornelius, "You are well aware that it is against our law for a Jew to associate with a Gentile or visit him." Despite the fact of the prayers by both Cornelius and Peter, and the visions these men had independent of each other, this had to have been a very awkward moment. A Jew coming into the home of a Gentile was a very rare activity. However, if reaching out to the "other sheep" is part of God's mission for His people and one's commitment to Jesus Christ, it will entail those times and moments where one has to step outside of one's heritage, customs and comfort zone. One will set aside his past traditions and literally step across a threshold into a place of God's assignment to minister to the "other sheep."

10. A Serious Defining Moment

It was said of John Wesley that he was committed to go anywhere, at any time, to do any work, at any cost. In the course of his ministry commitment, *Landmarks Magazine* for September 1997, had this observation of how and to whom John Wesley ministered. "Wesley's mission was largely to the laboring class of people but he was not indifferent to all other classes. His audiences included farmers, lawyers, clergymen and nonconformist ministers, university undergraduates and civic leaders as well as those from foreign lands, especially the Germans in Newcastle." This was the scope of the "other sheep" ministry done by John Wesley. It was the same scope of ministry into which Peter would be thrust with the Gospel. It is the same scope of ministry intensity for those of us who follow Jesus Christ. It is along the line of what Paul shared as his level of commitment in I Corinthians 9:19-22 (NIV), "Though I am free and belong to no man, I make myself a slave to everyone, to win as many as possible. To the Jews I became like a Jew, to win the Jews. To those under the law I became like one under the law…so as to win those under the law. To those not having the law I became like one not having the law…so as to win those not having the law. To the weak I became weak, to win the weak. I have become all things to all men so that by all possible means I might save some." The witness of Paul's desire to serve the Lord at all times is summarized in Romans 1:14-16 (NIV), "I am obligated both to Greeks and non-Greeks, both to the wise and the foolish. That is why I am so eager to preach the gospel also to you who are at Rome. I am not ashamed of the gospel, because it is the power of God for the salvation of everyone who believes: first for the Jew, then for the Gentile." The level of his commitment should be noticed and embraced: "I am obligated" and "I am so eager" and "I am not ashamed of the Gospel…" Is your level of commitment similar to Paul's? What a difference there would be if more were committed to serve with this motivation and dedication.

As Peter extended himself into this new horizon of ministry

to "other sheep," and as he proclaimed the Word of the Lord, we read about the impact of this ministry in Acts 10:44-48 (NIV), "While Peter was still speaking these words, the Holy Spirit came on all who heard the message. The circumcised believers who had come with Peter were astonished that the gift of the Holy Spirit had been poured out even on the Gentiles...Can anyone keep these people from being baptized with water? So he ordered that they be baptized in the name of Jesus Christ. Then they asked Peter to stay with them for a few days." One should never place limits or restrictions on what God can and will do. There are "other sheep" who must be reached for Jesus Christ. The Lord knows who and where they are and He wants us to be flexible and diligent in the task of finding them for Him. Can I do this ministry for Jesus Christ? How will I know where and to whom I should go? Will I have strength for the journey? The words to an old Chorus, written by Sidney E Cox, reminds one of this truth.

> My Lord knows the way through the wilderness,
> All I have to do is follow…
> Strength for today is mine all the way,
> And all that I need for tomorrow.
> My Lord knows the way through,
> All I have to do is follow.

Servants of Cornelius came seeking Peter to bring him back with them so he would have the opportunity of sharing the Gospel to a people group he had not considered beforehand. Peter, a Jew, would venture into a new area for ministry and enter the home of Cornelius, a Gentile. In a very general way, we have a sense of what was on the mind and heart of Jesus Christ as He ministered. Doubtlessly, the "little boats" and "little people" and "other sheep" were always part of what His ministry encompassed. We get an idea of this in Matthew 11:28-30 (NIV), where Jesus said, "Come to me, all you who are weary and burdened, and I will give you rest. Take my yoke upon you and learn from me, for I am gentle and humble in heart, and you will find rest for your souls. For my yoke is easy and my burden is light." *The Message Paraphrase* has taken some liberty with this text and has an interesting rendering of this passage, "Are you tired? Worn out? Burned out on religion? Come to me. Get away with me and you'll recover your life. I'll show you how to take a real rest. Walk with me and work with me - watch how I do it. Learn the unforced rhythms of grace. I won't lay anything heavy or ill-fitting on you. Keep company with me and you'll learn to live freely and lightly." In Matthew 11:29, Jesus has said, "Take my yoke upon you and learn from me, for I am gentle and humble in heart, and you will find rest for your souls." What is it to take the yoke of Christ upon you and to learn from Jesus? Is it merely that He is gentle and humble in heart and that He wants His followers and servants to be like Him? Is this the only pathway for one to find rest and peace for his or her soul?

The yoke suggests several things. It means the one who is to be yoked is to be controlled. It also means one must be teamed together with someone else. By definition, it is "a device for joining together a pair of draft animals, especially oxen, usually consisting of a crosspiece with two bow-shaped pieces, each enclosing the head of an animal." In A. T. Robertson's *Word Pictures of the New Testament*, his translation of "yoke" is: "The rabbis used yoke to mean school. The English word "school" is Greek for leisure. But Jesus offers refreshment in his school and promises to make the burden light, for he is a meek and humble teacher. Humility was not a virtue among the ancients. It was ranked with servility. Jesus has made a virtue of this vice. He has glorified this attitude so that Paul urges it (Philippians 2:3) "in lowliness of mind each counting other better than himself." In portions of modern day Europe, people place yokes on the shoulders to make the burden easier to carry. Jesus promises we shall learn His yoke is kindly (easy) and the burden lightened by His help. The yoke of Christ is useful, good, and kindly."

If we are in the School of Jesus Christ and we are learning about Him, what exactly are we supposed to learn and how obvious will it be that we have met His standard for our lives and His service? What we learn and who we are will make a great difference to the "little boats, little people and other sheep." We begin by learning that Jesus Christ is meek and lowly. This means we are to be like Him as we take His yoke upon us. This is an important lesson one should learn in the classroom of Jesus. There are other areas for consideration. If one is to be like Jesus and under His control, then Colossians 3:8-11 (NIV) must become part of one's life and lifestyle. In the text, we learn, "But now you must rid yourselves of all such things as these: anger, rage, malice, slander, and filthy language from your lips. Do not lie to each other, since you have taken off your old self with its practices and have put on the new self, which is being renewed in knowledge in the image of its Creator. Here there is no Greek or Jew, circumcised or uncircumcised, barbarian, Scythian, slave or free, but Christ is all, and is in all."

The first major lesson is to be "renewed in knowledge in the image of your Creator." That knowledge teaches one that there has to be a transformation in one's life as particular negatives are gotten rid of, such as, "Anger, rage, malice, slander, and filthy language." It is a radical and transforming change as the old self is taken off and the new self has been put on. The positives of the new self are given in Colossians 3:12-15 (NIV), "Therefore, as God's chosen people, holy and dearly loved, clothe yourselves with compassion, kindness, humility, gentleness and patience. Bear with each other and forgive whatever grievances you may have against one another. Forgive as the Lord forgave you. And over all these virtues put on love, which binds them all together in perfect unity. Let the peace of Christ rule in your hearts, since as members of one body you were called to peace. And be thankful." Has this transformation occurred in your life? Is some evidence of a spiritual schizophrenia or dichotomy lurking within you? Is the old self and new self-struggling for control in your life? As you try to progress with the new self, does the vocabulary and attitude of the old self intrude and thwart your growth and progress in your spiritual learning process?

As one wrestles with the old while coming under the control of the yoke of Jesus, Ephesians 4:20-24 (NIV) shares with us that, "You were taught, with regard to your former way of life, to put off your old self, which is being corrupted by its deceitful desires; to be made new in the attitude of your minds; and to put on the new self, created to be like God in true righteousness and holiness." We learn in the school of Jesus that we are to be "renewed in knowledge in the image of the Creator." In addition, we are instructed that we are "created to be like God in true righteousness and holiness." While we are focused on the implications of what it means to have the knowledge, righteousness and holiness of The Creator, we have other concerns and behavior modifications that are occurring simultaneously. In Ephesians 4:25-32 (NIV) we are instructed, "Therefore each of you must put off falsehood and speak truthfully to his neighbor, for we are all members of one body. In your anger do not sin: Do not let the sun go down while you are still angry, and do not give the devil a foothold. He who has been stealing must steal no longer, but must work, doing something useful with his own hands, that he may have something to share with those in need. Do not let any unwholesome talk come out of your mouths, but only what is helpful for building others up according to their needs, that it may benefit those who listen. And do not grieve the Holy Spirit of God, with whom you were sealed for the day of redemption. Get rid of all bitterness, rage and anger, brawling and slander, along with every form of malice. Be kind and compassionate to one another, forgiving each other, just as in Christ God forgave you."

One small word that many fail to see or try to overlook is the word "all." The instruction and direction is never to get rid of "some" negative behaviors. It is always "all" negatives must go and "all" positives must fill the vacuum in one's life and lifestyle. It is interesting to note "all" is part of the appeal of Jesus in Matthew 11 when He said, "Come to Me, all who are weary and heavy-burdened." When Jesus invites "all," He expects us to do the same. He did not indicate "some" but "all"! That is what He said and that is what He meant. It is a sad and regrettable admission when we have to acknowledge that The Church is not always the best place to see the new behaviors modeled. It's almost prophetic that the words of Charles H. Spurgeon are the experience in many places that are called Church! He said, "A time will come when instead of shepherds feeding the sheep, the church will have clowns entertaining the goats." We may have arrived at that place.

APPLICATIONS and QUESTIONS:

How flexible are you when it comes to "doing" ministry versus talking about what ought to be done?

If you were alive in Peter's day shared in his background training, how readily would you have responded to the request of a Gentile?

How readily do you respond in your community to and with those who look different or act differently in your community?
Are you concerned about where they will spend eternity?

If one was seeking new life in Christ and came to "The Church" you presently attend, would they find the "new self" behaviors being lived out in the lives of the members? What about your life? What would they see in you that would cause them to seek Jesus Christ?

10. A Serious Defining Moment

If you had to evaluate and score where you are in terms of the "old self" and the "new self", would you receive a passing grade? Why?

What three directives of the "new self" behaviors do you find to be the most challenging or most difficult for you? Why?

> *Art thou weary, heavy-laden, Art thou sore distressed?*
> *Come to Me, saith One, and coming, Be at rest.*
>
> *Hath He marks to lead me to Him, If He be my Guide?*
> *In His feet and hands are wound prints And His side.*
>
> *Finding, following, keeping, struggling, Is He sure to bless?*
> *Saints, apostles, prophets, martyrs, Answer, Yes!*
>
> Stephen of Mar Saba

11. A Serious Possibility

A person is wise to think about and have in place a Life-Plan. The purpose of higher education is to prepare one for some specialty field of interest. It can be in the field of teaching, medicine, law, ministry, science, aerospace and a host of other fields of endeavor. After finding one's place in the specialty field, one then plans for the future with savings, investments, health and life insurance, home ownership and other practical considerations. Regardless of how well one's life-plan is set in place, there are always some unknowns that can occur suddenly and without too much advance warning. Not long ago in our community, a young and very active woman had a stroke. It was sudden and proved to be fatal. Within a few days, she went from very active to being buried. Our military, training Afghans how to defend and protect their country, are shot and killed by their trainee. Those who are among the multitudes of Wounded Warriors from both the Iraq and Afghanistan wars can rehearse how the unexpected could occur. Suddenly and unexpectedly, their life-plan took on a new dimension and focus.

In the area of finance, there are countless numbers of people who lost their income because of economic issues that caused them to lose their home through foreclosure, and saw their savings reduced sharply due to money markets and investments that failed rather than increased in value. It may take years before one can regain some of what was lost. With all of the shifts, changes and possibilities that occur in one's life, there should be a remembrance of "the other little boats, little people and the other sheep" who are trapped by their situation or environment. Too often, they are among those who have no life-plan and are more helpless than others. Regardless of what occurs, their plight is such that they offer

11. A Serious Possibility

little or no resistance. Some people become so desperate that they do what is contrary to their normal behavior and moral values. During December 2014, a woman became so desperate to get some food for her children who had gone three days with no food, she attempted to steal three eggs so they would have something to eat. The police officer dispatched to the scene of the theft demonstrated mercy rather than justice by providing food for her hungry family. With a nation becoming more indebted and gainful employment becoming more difficult to find, we may see and hear of more desperate activity and theft.

War can dramatically change one's life-plan. It's not just being wounded in conflict, but also coming under the control of a hostile government. There is an interesting section in the book, *Unbroken*, written by Laura Hillenbrand. The setting of the book ranges from the Berlin Olympics in 1936 into World War II up to 1945. A summary statement contains the following, "During WW II, only one in every 100 Americans captured in Europe died…nearly one in three perished while in Japanese captivity. You will recall the earlier mention of the book Unbroken that it is the remarkable tale of Louis Silvie Zamperini, a world-class runner who competed in the 1936 Berlin Summer Olympics and who later became a WW II B-24 Bombardier in the Pacific Theater. In late May 1943, Zamperini's plane, the Green Hornet, goes down in the Pacific Ocean while (ironically) searching for a missing plane. He, along with his pilot and one other man, endure more than a 7 week/2000 mile ordeal (the longest in recorded history). They are "lost at sea on a fragile raft with no water or food, as a frenzy of expectant sharks persistently encircled the fading men, rubbing their backs against the raft and occasionally lunging up onto it only to later have Louie and his pilot (the 3rd man died) captured by the Japanese and to spend the next two years in multiple Prisoner of War camps and subjected to a whole new set of tortures." Hillenbrand writes: "…the guards sought to deprive them of something that had sustained them even as all else had been lost: dignity. This self-respect and sense of self-worth, the innermost armament of the soul, lies at the heart of humanness; to be deprived of it is to be dehumanized, to be cleaved from, and cast below, mankind. Men subjected to dehumanizing treatment experience profound wretchedness and loneliness, and find that hope is almost impossible to retain. Without dignity, identity is erased. In its absence, men are defined not by themselves, but by their captors and the circumstances in which they are forced to live" (Page 182). If the situation with the Japanese in World War II was effective and men were "dehumanized," can one be reprogrammed, reoriented and restored to a former "human" status? The description given that, "Men subjected to dehumanizing treatment experience profound wretchedness and loneliness, and find that hope is almost impossible to retain. Without dignity, identity is erased. In its absence, men are defined not by themselves, but by their captors and the circumstances in which they are forced to live." Can this condition be reversed and the man be restored to his former state and status? There may be no acceptable physical and psychological answer for this type of condition.

There are all different methods employed to "brainwash" or to "reorient" a person to have a different thought process instilled regarding their captivity and captors. One method that is effective in the short-term is known as Stockholm Syndrome. "Stockholm Syndrome, or capture-bonding, is a psychological phenomenon in which hostages express empathy and have positive feelings towards their captors, sometimes to the point of defending them. These feelings are generally considered irrational in light of the danger or risk endured by the victims, who essentially mistake a lack of abuse from their captors for an act of kindness. The FBI's Hostage Barricade Database System shows that roughly 27% of victims show evidence of Stockholm Syndrome. Stockholm Syndrome can be seen as a form of traumatic bonding, which does not necessarily require a hostage scenario, but which describes strong emotional ties that develop between two persons where one person intermittently harasses, beats, threatens, abuses, or intimidates the other."

The Bible records different instances where the captor tried to reorient and indoctrinate the captive with the emphases being upon the customs, religion, and literature of the captor nation. The classic example is The Book of Daniel. The concept of reorientation and indoctrination is given in Daniel 1:3-7 (NIV), "Then the king ordered the chief of his court officials, to bring in some of the Israelites from the royal family and the nobility. They were to be young men without any physical defect, handsome, showing aptitude for every kind of learning, well informed, quick to understand, and qualified to serve in the king's palace. He was to teach them the language and literature of the Babylonians. The king assigned them a daily amount of food and wine from the king's table. They were to be trained for three years, and after that they were to enter the king's service. Among these were some from Judah: Daniel, Hananiah, Mishael and Azariah. The chief official gave them new names: to Daniel, the name Belteshazzar; to Hananiah, the name Shadrach; to Mishael, the name Meshach; and to Azariah, the name Abednego." These select young men were supposed to learn a new language, study new literature, consume a new diet of food and become accustomed to their new names. After three years, the reorientation will be completed and they will be found competent to be part of the king's service. This was the plan and objective. Would it succeed? Would these young men succumb to their reorientation and indoctrination? It could have and should have worked. What thwarted this reorientation and indoctrination plan?

The king and those in charge of the reorientation and indoctrination failed to consider one thing about these young men. They had been "trained up in the way they should go, so that when they were old, they would not depart from it" (Proverbs 22:6, NKJV). Daniel and his friends were men of purpose and commitment. They had foundational principles and core values that they would not compromise. It is not surprising then to read in Daniel 1:8-13 (NIV), "But Daniel resolved not to defile himself with the royal food and wine, and he asked the chief official for permission not to defile himself this way. Now God had caused the official to show favor and sympathy to Daniel, but the official told Daniel, I am afraid of my lord the king, who has assigned your food and drink. Why should he see you looking worse than the other young men your age? The king would then have my head because of you. Daniel then said to the guard whom the chief official had appointed over Daniel, Hananiah, Mishael and Azariah, please test your servants for ten days: Give us nothing but vegetables to eat and water to drink. Then compare our appearance with that of the young men who eat the royal food, and treat your servants in accordance with what you see."

Daniel and his friends offered a reasonable alternative to the king's demand. There was an element of risk in doing so but principles and values cannot be looked upon as having a chameleon characteristic that frequently changes determined by location and environment. It might be said that Daniel and his friends were "true blue" and would not change to any other color for any reason. Can any good result occur when a king's edict is not being followed? Can the best reasonable alternative assuage a king who expects compliance to his every desire, word and whim? The result after ten days could not be denied. Daniel 1:15-17 (NIV) records, "At the end of the ten days they looked healthier and better nourished than any of the young men who ate the royal food. So the guard took away their choice food and the wine they were to drink and gave them vegetables instead. To these four young men God gave knowledge and understanding of all kinds of literature and learning. And Daniel could understand visions and dreams of all kinds."

Their commitment to no surrender and no compromise was honored by the Lord. They now had a new mission in a new place and their foundational principles and core values would preserve them throughout their captivity and ordeal. Interestingly, they would have unique opportunities to represent The Lord in a foreign and hostile place.

When one thinks about captivity and degrees of mind control employed, is there a recommendation one can suggest that might result in a partial or complete recovery of the captive once he is released? Is it possible for one to be released but not yet free from the rudiments of the incarceration? Is there any hope and possibility of change for the former captive? The basic biblical description of humankind is that man was created as one who possesses a body and soul and spirit. A starting place would be in the prayer offered by Paul to the Church at Thessalonica, (I Thessalonians 5:23-24 (NIV), "May God himself, the God of peace, sanctify you through and through. May your whole spirit, soul and body be kept blameless at the coming of our Lord Jesus Christ. The one who calls you is faithful and he will do it." It is the portion of the prayer, "May your whole spirit, soul and body be kept blameless" that offers hope and possibility for restoration and renewal in spirit, soul and body. The other aspect of this hope and possibility comes from II Corinthians 5:17-18 (NIV), "Therefore, if anyone is in Christ, he is a new creation; the old has gone, the new has come! All this is from God, who reconciled us to himself through Christ..." Will this new creation in one's soul, also benefit one's body and spirit? God created man as a totality and is unlimited in the new creation work that He will bring to pass. God is a God of love, mercy and grace. He is a God of compassion. He is fully capable to renew, revive and restore anyone at any time. The very fact of who God is fills one with hope, confidence and possibility. God will cause all things to work together for one's good, for those who are called according to His purpose (Romans 8:28-30). The words in Jeremiah 29:11

(NASB) speak to the possibilities of renewed hope and purpose, "'For I know the plans that I have for you, declares the Lord, plans for welfare and not for calamity to give you a future and a hope." The only unknown is how, when and where He will use one according to His purpose. A stanza of the hymn written by Charles Wesley, "And Can It Be That I Should Gain?" includes these powerful words:

> Long my imprisoned spirit lay,
> Fast bound in sin and nature's night;
> Thine eye diffused a quickening ray—
> I woke, the dungeon flamed with light;
> My chains fell off, my heart was free,
> I rose, went forth, and followed Thee.
> My chains fell off, my heart was free,
> I rose, went forth, and followed Thee.
> Amazing love! How can it be,
> That Thou, my God, shouldest die for me?

That which is true for the soul of man, offers hope and possibility for the body and spirit of man as well. Man's whole body, soul and spirit can be transformed and fashioned by the Grace of God in accordance with the will of God for the new creature in Christ Jesus.

How would you react if you became a captive and were expected to comply with the directives of your captors? As an illustration, let us insert ourselves in the time-frame when Peter wrote his epistles. Our identity would be with those in I Peter 1:1-2 (NIV), "Peter, an apostle of Jesus Christ, To God's elect, strangers in the world, scattered throughout Pontus, Galatia, Cappadocia, Asia and Bithynia, who have been chosen according to the foreknowledge of God the Father, through the sanctifying work of the Spirit, for obedience to Jesus Christ and sprinkling by his blood:

Grace and peace be yours in abundance?" Our identity would be "strangers in the world" who were being "scattered" throughout surrounding regions. We would be under attack and there would be those who were seeking to imprison or kill us. What would you do? Where would you go? What about all of your stuff (possessions)? Would you leave it or try to take it with you? What about your dignity? Would you fight to preserve and maintain it, or realize it is slowly ebbing away? Would you be like a character in *Fiddler on the Roof*?

The storyline of *Fiddler on the Roof* is rather simple. "The family of Tevye, is a Jewish family living in the town of Anatevka, in Tsarist Russia, in 1905. Anatevka is broken into two sections: a small Orthodox Jewish section; and a larger Orthodox Christian section. Tevye notes that, 'We don't bother them, and so far, they don't bother us.' Tevye is not wealthy, despite working hard, like most Jews in Anatevka, also having many children. Life in the little town of Anatevka is very hard and Tevye speaks not only of the difficulties of being poor but also of the Jewish community's constant fear of harassment from their non-Jewish neighbors" (Summary copied from Wikipedia). The time comes when they have to leave their village and home. It will be difficult and dangerous. They carry as much of their possessions for their arduous journey. The unanswered question is: Will they survive the journey toward an uncertain destination? Will their possessions be an asset or a hindrance for them on this journey?

Peter states in his epistle that the journey will be difficult and painful. In I Peter 4:12-15 (NIV), he instructs the scattered believers, "Dear friends, do not be surprised at the painful trial you are suffering, as though something strange were happening to you. But rejoice that you participate in the sufferings of Christ, so that you may be overjoyed when his glory is revealed. If you are insulted because of the name of Christ, you are blessed, for the Spirit of glory and of God rests on you. If you suffer, it should not be as a murderer or thief or any other kind of criminal, or even as a meddler. However, if you suffer as a Christian, do not be ashamed, but praise God that you bear that name." This insertion into the timeframe of Peter's Epistles asks, how well do you like the prospect of what that entailed? How well would you survive? What priorities would be foremost for you? If you were being scattered, what direction would be most feasible? Where would you go? Who would you be able to trust? Would you forget about or neglect to consider the plight of the "little boats, little people and other sheep" in the midst of the chaos and suffering? Who will demonstrate care and concern for them? Will they be viewed as inconsequential and insignificant at such a crucial and critical time?

Let us insert Matthew 24:14-22 (NIV) into our thinking. Consider the intensity of the day described by Jesus Christ. "And this gospel of the kingdom will be preached in the whole world as a testimony to all nations, and then the end will come. So when you see standing in the holy place 'the abomination that causes desolation,' spoken of through the prophet Daniel, let the reader understand, then let those who are in Judea flee to the mountains. Let no one on the roof of his house go down to take anything out of the house. Let no one in the field go back to get his cloak. How dreadful it will be in those days for pregnant women and nursing mothers! Pray that your flight will not take place in winter or on the Sabbath. For then there will be great distress, unequaled from the beginning of the world until now--and never to be equaled again. If those days had not been cut short, no one would survive, but for the sake of the elect those days will be shortened."

These events are significantly different from the average Life-Plan of most people. The level of expectation does not even contemplate the hard times mentioned in Scripture. In Matthew 24:4-13 (NIV), even though Jesus gave a cautionary word and warning, many have not contemplated what it means or how it could impact them personally. The words of Jesus are, "Watch out that no one deceives you. For many will come in my name, claiming, I am the Christ, and will deceive many. You will hear of wars and rumors of wars, but see to it that you are not alarmed. Such things must happen, but the end is still to come. Nation will rise against nation, and kingdom against kingdom. There will be famines and earthquakes in various places. All these are the beginning of birth pains. Then you will be handed over to be persecuted and put to death, and you will be hated by all nations because of me. At that time many will turn away from the faith and will betray and hate each other, and many false prophets will appear and deceive many people. Because of the increase of wickedness, the love of most will grow cold, but he who stands firm to the end will be saved."

With biblical teaching and doctrine, it would be unwise to assume the characteristic attributed to the ostrich by putting one's head into the sand. It may prevent what one sees but there is a large part of the Ostrich still exposed to danger and peril. I'm aware that some interpret these events of having already occurred, or that the Church will be raptured before they occur, etc. One must remember the context of this discussion by Jesus. In Matthew 24:1-3 (NIV), Jesus left the temple and was walking away when his disciples came up to him to call his attention to its buildings. "Do you see all these things, He asked? I tell you the truth, not one stone here will be left on another; everyone will be thrown down." As Jesus was sitting on the Mount of Olives, the disciples came to him privately. "Tell us, they said, when will this happen, and what will be the sign of Your coming and of the end of the age?" The two questions Jesus was asked was, what will be the sign of your coming and what will be the sign of the end of the age? Jesus draws a very grim picture as He responds to events that will occur and engulf people. The timing for these events is couched in the following terms, Matthew 24:42-44 (NIV), "Therefore keep watch, because you do not know on what day your Lord will come. But understand this: If the owner of the house had known at what time of night the thief was coming, he would have kept watch and would not have let his house be broken into. So you also must be ready, because the Son of Man will come at an hour when you do not expect him."

The times in which we live are changing rapidly. One of the places of considerable change is the removal of God from the everyday life of the nation and the affairs of State. The political conventions of the Republicans and Democrats were held in 2012 to go through the process of nominating the candidates of their choice to contend for the office of president. For the Republican Convention, representatives of the Mormon Church were invited to give a Prayer, along with Cardinal Timothy Dolan of the Roman Catholic Church. In the Democratic Convention, Cardinal Dolan had offered to give a Prayer but his offer was declined. The Blaze and The Drudge Report posted: "The host committee for the Democratic National Convention has raised a number of eyebrows after choosing to proceed with featuring Islamic "Jumah" prayers for two hours on the Friday of its convention, though Democrats earlier denied a Catholic Cardinal's request to say a prayer at the same event (they relented and extended an Invitation for Cardinal Dolan to give The Benediction)." Does this represent a credible and viable illustration of, "What will be the sign of Your coming and of the end of the age?" Is the Islamic Prayer at an American political convention included in the response of Jesus regarding last days and end times?

In all of these considerations and possibilities, what about the "little boats, little people and the other sheep" who are caught up in, and maybe victims of the cultural war? What is the Culture War and what impact and effect will occur in this nation? Have we become a nation and world where we see classes of people rather than individuals trying to navigate on the sea of life? Are most people viewed as being insignificant, and an elite class emerging as being more significant? If we are heading in that direction, what will happen to the majority of "little boats, little people and other sheep"? Will they, in effect, be allowed to sink, or die, or be scattered to unknown and unsafe places?

Wikipedia has the following statement defining the Culture Wars. "The expression was reintroduced in the 1991 publication of *Culture Wars: The Struggle to Define America* by James Davison Hunter, a sociologist at the University of Virginia. Hunter described what he saw as a dramatic realignment and polarization that had transformed American politics and culture. He argued that on an increasing number of hot-button defining issues, such as, abortion, gun control politics, separation of church and state, privacy, recreational drug use, homosexuality, censorship issues, there existed two definable polarities. Furthermore, not only were there a number of divisive issues, but society had divided along essentially the same lines on these issues, so as to constitute two warring groups, defined primarily not by nominal religion, ethnicity, social class, or even political affiliation, but rather by ideological world views. Hunter characterized this polarity as stemming from opposite impulses, toward what he referred to as Progressivism and Orthodoxy.

In 1990, commentator Pat Buchanan mounted a campaign for the Republican nomination for the office of President of the United States against incumbent President George H. W. Bush to be held in November 1992. During his speech, he declared, "There is a religious war going on in our country for the soul of America. It is a cultural war, as critical to the kind of nation we will one day be as was the Cold War itself. In addition to criticizing environmental extremists and radical feminism, he said public morality was a defining issue." Some of the casualties and victims of the culture war are those who are trapped in the quagmire of our times. The "other little boats" are unable to navigate the troubled seas on their own. The "little people" have difficulty being networked to and with those who can articulate and frame the argument in the debate and culture war battleground. The "other sheep" are easily scattered and become prey for the predators that are lurking and eager to seize the helpless and vulnerable. The culture war is relentless and constant. In a 2004 column in The *American Conservative Magazine*, Pat Buchanan wrote, "The culture war had reignited and that certain groups of Americans no longer inhabited the same moral universe." He gave such examples as same-sex civil unions, the crudity of the MTV crowd, and the controversy surrounding Mel Gibson's film *The Passion of the Christ*. He wrote: "Who is in your face here? Who started this? Who is on the offensive? Who is pushing the envelope? The answer is obvious. A radical Left aided by a cultural elite that detests Christianity and finds Christian moral tenets reactionary and repressive is bent on pushing its amoral values and imposing its ideology on our nation. The wisdom of what the Hollywood and the Left are about should be transparent to all."

Has the culture improved any since these comments were written in 2004 or has the Culture remained in steady decline and deterioration? One would be hard-put to locate and demonstrate any improvement. Most of the available literature indicates there is no improvement and states that there is further erosion of the remaining values and wealth of the nation. The thought of some is that this nation will implode one day soon. In a book review and news item, World Net Daily, August 29, 2012, contains the following: "At a time of skyrocketing federal debt, declining morality and growing spiritual apathy and apostasy, New York Times bestselling author Joel C. Rosenberg, known as a modern-day Nostradamus, says America may face cataclysmic collapse in the not-too distant future." In his new book, *Implosion: Can America Recover from its Economic and Spiritual Challenges in Time?* "Rosenberg explores the question a growing number of politicians, academics, authors and others who are asking about the future of the United States of America. My concern is we are experiencing an epic failure of leadership at almost every level of American society right now. Something has gone terribly wrong with the American experiment. Our families are imploding, our national debt is exploding, experts on the left and right are warning us that we need to change our direction because we're on an unsustainable trajectory economically, socially and culturally. Unfortunately, too many leaders in our country are stuck in the business as usual mode and Americans are getting anxious that the ice is cracking under our feet." Is this a valid concern? Have we actually stepped over the threshold onto the slippery slope? Are we beginning to accelerate downward with no ability to slow or stop our descent? Have we become irretrievable as a nation and unredeemable as a people? Has God given us up to our foolish and sinful ways?

Let us consider the last question above, "Has God given us up to our foolish and sinful ways?" with Romans 1:18-32 (NLT), "But God shows his anger from heaven against all sinful, wicked people who push the truth away from themselves. For the truth about God is known to them instinctively. God has put this knowledge in their hearts. From the time the world was created, people have seen the earth and sky and all that God made. They can clearly see His invisible qualities, His eternal power and divine nature. So they have no excuse whatsoever for not knowing God. Yes, they knew God, but they wouldn't worship Him as God or even give Him thanks. And they began to think up foolish ideas of what God was like. The result was that their minds became dark and confused. Claiming to be wise, they became utter fools instead. And instead of worshiping the glorious, ever-living God, they worshiped idols made to look like mere people, or birds and animals and snakes. So God let them go ahead and do whatever shameful things their hearts desired. As a result, they did vile and degrading things with each other's bodies. Instead of believing what they knew was the truth about God, they deliberately chose to believe lies. So they worshiped the things God made but not the Creator himself, who is to be praised forever. That is why God abandoned them to their shameful desires. Even the women turned against the natural way to have sex and instead indulged in sex with each other. And the men, instead of having normal sexual relationships with women, burned with lust for each other. Men did shameful things with other men and, as a result, suffered within themselves the penalty they so richly deserved. When they refused to acknowledge God, He abandoned them to their evil minds and let them do things that should never be done. Their lives became full of every kind of wickedness, sin, greed, hate, envy, murder, fighting, deception, malicious behavior, and gossip. They are backstabbers, haters of God, insolent, proud, and boastful. They are forever inventing new ways of sinning and are disobedient to their parents. They refuse to understand, break their promises, and are heartless and unforgiving. They are fully aware of God's death penalty for those who do these things, yet they go right ahead and do them anyway. And, worse yet, they encourage others to do them, too."

Does this describe who we are becoming as a nation, or have we already arrived at that place of God's condemnation? If we look at the culture of our time and the behavior of increasing numbers of our population, it becomes easy to conclude that we have arrived as a nation into this abyss of rebellion against God. While we still have the opportunity, we need to do all we can to rescue and safely secure those who are existing as "the other little boats, the little people and the other sheep." We can do it! We need to do it now! No one should be viewed as expendable, inconsequential or insignificant.

APPLICATIONS and QUESTIONS:

If you were taken captive by an enemy or other nation, and were told never to mention the name of God or Jesus Christ, what would you do?

In consideration of Acts 20:24 (ESV), "But I do not account my life of any value nor as precious to myself, if only I may finish my course and the ministry that I received from the Lord Jesus, to testify to the gospel of the grace of God." What should you be willing to do?

In consideration of Philippians 1:20-21 (ESV), "As it is my eager expectation and hope that I will not be at all ashamed, but that with full courage now as always Christ will be honored in my body, whether by life or by death. For to me to live is Christ, and to die is gain." How should you function and behave even when times are hard and uncertain?

What should your level of urgency be regarding the "little boats, little people and other sheep"? Do you see them as being expendable, inconsequential or insignificant? If so, why?

Who should be engaged with a sense of urgency and effort? What if no one else in the Church was concerned or interested, should that negate or terminate the urgency for you?

Should you have any involvement or concern for the victims of war and how it may have affected them? How would you relate to one with that experience?

What would you purpose to do for one who is labeled or categorized as hopeless? Is that person beyond the reach of God's grace? Is God able to redeem, restore, renew and revive the hopeless soul?

Only one life to offer, Jesus, my Lord and King;
Only one tongue to praise Thee And of Thy mercy sing (forever);
Only one heart's devotion, Savior, O may it be
Consecrated alone to Thy matchless glory, Yielded fully to Thee.

Only this hour is mine, Lord, May it be used for Thee;
May every passing moment Count for eternity (my Savior);
Souls all about are dying, Dying in sin and shame;
Help me bring them the message of Calvary's redemption
In Thy glorious name.

Only one life to offer, Take it, dear Lord, I pray;
Nothing from Thee withholding, Thy will I now obey (my Jesus);
Thou who hast freely given Thine all in all for me,
Claim this life for Thine own, to be used, my Savior,
Every moment for Thee.

Avis Marguerite Burgeson Christiansen

12. A Serious Acknowledgement

The Christian Life has basic foundational principles and core values. One of the most basic guideline and instruction is Proverbs 3:3-7 (ESV), "Let not steadfast love and faithfulness forsake you; bind them around your neck; write them on the tablet of your heart. So you will find favor and good success in the sight of God and man. Trust in the Lord with all your heart, and do not lean on your own understanding. In all your ways acknowledge him, and he will make straight your paths. Be not wise in your own eyes; fear the Lord, and turn away from evil." The key phrase for our focus is, "In all your ways, acknowledge Him." Simply stated, God is to have first place, the preeminence, the priority in each one who desires Him and His will for his or her life. "Acknowledge" has several possible translations. One of them is, we are to "clearly understand" God. It means to be "aware" and "informed" about Who God is and how one can revere and honor Him. The one thing that all have in common, whether a big boat or a little boat, whether a prominent person or an obscure one, whether a sheep within the fold or one yet to be adopted into the flock, all of us have to arrive at the point where in all our ways we "acknowledge Him." There are no exceptions and no exemptions.

In 1981, a book was published by Rabbi Harold Kushner. A Critique by Dr. Norman Geisler followed and contains the following, "Until the premature death of his son from progeria (rapid aging), Rabbi Harold Kushner believed, as many do, that God was all-good and all powerful. This tragic death caused a reexamination of these traditional beliefs and resulted in the publication of his best-selling book, "When Bad Things Happen to Good People." Using the book of Job as a background, Rabbi Kushner suggests there are three things all of us would like to believe: (1) God is all-powerful and causes everything that happens; (2) God is just and fair, giving everyone what they deserve; (3) Job is a good person. As long as Job is healthy and happy one can believe in all three of these. But in view of Job's righteous suffering, Rabbi Kushner concludes we cannot hold both to 1 and 2. For no good person should be subjected to such terrible misfortunes as was Job."

The Rabbi was an interesting man to hear and his book caused many to think through their own view of God and the mental picture one has of Him. The bottom line is whether or not God is to be acknowledged only when things are going in a positive direction. If the negatives begin to occur and multiply, the temptation and tendency is to resort to a human rationale and seek a logical conclusion for the occurrence of the negatives. That type of thinking would cause one to avoid a key part of Proverbs 3:6, namely, "in ALL things ACKNOWLEDGE HIM." One needs to guard against substituting "some" for the "all". If one takes the "all things" of Proverbs 3:6 and lays them alongside the words in Romans 8:28 (NKJV), a clear understanding should be present. "And we know that ALL things work together for good to those who love God, to those who are the called according to His purpose." If one takes the "all things" in Proverbs 3:6 and the "all things" in Romans 8:28, it is obvious that they are one and the same. The "all things" may include some things one deems to be negative and hurtful in the present. In the bigger picture of God's plan for one's life, the "all things" are part of the "good things" God has in store for those who love Him and are called according to His purpose. These truths about God need to be declared to all, including the "little boats, little people and the other sheep." We need to avoid a timid approach about these truths and declare them boldly and thoroughly. They are foundational and the basis for one's hope. They enable one to endure and to be comforted by the fact of God's eternal and perfect plan for one's good and one's life.

An inescapable fact is that we live in a broken world. Un

fairness and discord, fear and pain are a very real part of our daily lives. The unexpected can occur and alter one's life significantly. It reminds one of an event in the life of Mark Thallander on August 3, 2003. Mark was an acclaimed musician with exceptional skill on the organ and piano. He also had unique ability with writing and composing music for these instruments. The narrative regarding an event on August 3, 2003 that would alter his life dramatically is shared on his own website: "It started off like just about any other Sunday...This Sunday he was teaming up with a friend from college...they worked together seamlessly as they led the congregation in a service of worship in song...They spent the afternoon together celebrating reunited friendships with several people, reminiscing for hours. Before he realized it, Mark noticed it was past time for him to make his journey back to his host's home in Maine, just over 100 miles away...As he headed back in the (borrowed) Toyota...Mark very quickly realized that his Sunday drive through the beautiful New England countryside would not be the normal picturesque drive down winding roads through rolling hills of lush green trees. Instead he would be enjoying another New England phenomenon, the summer storm...Approaching his exit to complete his journey to Gary's (His Host's) house, Mark lost control of the 4Runner, hit the guardrail, tossing him violently around the cab and landing him in the oncoming traffic...Mark explained to the doctors that he was an organist and pianist and really needed them to save his arm. They whisked him into surgery... As Mark awoke after surgery, Gary told him they had amputated his arm. And a new journey began..."

Was this event in the life of Mark Thallander a bad thing happening to a good person? For one who had dedicated his life and talent to Church music and ministry, where was God at this moment of crisis? Was this God's way of saying this person had served Him long enough? What would Mark do with the rest of his life? Can God still use a one-armed organist and pianist? Following

12. A Serious Acknowledgement

his recovery, the narrative continues about his participation in a friend's concert, "Mark...can make more music with one arm and two feet than most of us ever could with two arms and two feet...he sat down to play an amazing fantasia on the joyful, joyful theme. With his one hand he flew up and down...the keyboard and usually took the melody in the pedals. It was an arrangement he had done himself and it was amazing. Everyone was completely still, most with mouths wide open, many with eyes full of tears. Mark's was a strong testimony of the grace of God in the lives of his saints: that this fine organist could lose an arm and go through so many hard times, and still play this Joyful, Joyful as if he meant it..." (Read the entire story at: http://www.markthallander.com/story/index.asp). A stanza from a hymn contains an appropriate reminder and a word of encouragement,

> Be still, my soul: the hour is hastening on
> When we shall be forever with the Lord.
> When disappointment, grief, and fear are gone,
> Sorrow forgot, love's purest joys restored.
> by Catharina von Schlegel (1752)

Some people respond in a crisis situation with a question, "Where was God when the Tsunami occurred in Japan (2004)?" "Where was God when Katrina came to Louisiana (2005)?" "Where was God when the earthquake and after shocks brought such devastation to Haiti (2010)?" "Where is God when I need Him most?" Someone gave an answer that sounds terse, but it was not intended to be understood in that way. Their response to, "Where was God...?" states that God was in the same place where He was when Jesus was beaten, falsely accused, and crucified. God was observing the anguish and suffering of His Son. Isaiah 53:11 (ESV) records, "Out of the anguish of his soul he shall see and be satisfied; by his knowledge shall the righteous one, my servant, make many to be accounted righteous, and he shall bear their iniquities." It was at this point that propitiation and expiation was taking place because of our sins. Propitiation means the turning away of wrath by an offering. It means placating or satisfying the wrath of God by the atoning sacrifice of Christ. Expiation emphasizes the removal of guilt through a payment of the penalty, while propitiation emphasizes the appeasement or averting of God's wrath and justice. Both words are related to reconciliation, since it is through the death of Christ on the cross for our sins that we are reconciled to our God. This was part of an eternal plan. In I Peter 1:18-21 (NKJV), "Knowing that you were not redeemed with corruptible things, like silver or gold, from your aimless conduct received by tradition from your fathers, but with the precious blood of Christ, as of a lamb without blemish and without spot. He indeed was foreordained before the foundation of the world, but was manifest in these last times for you who through Him believe in God, who raised Him from the dead and gave Him glory, so that your faith and hope are in God." That which was "manifest in these last times" to us who believe had been known and determined "before the foundation of the world."

In like manner, one's life in this world is part of an eternal plan as well. We don't live in a vacuum and things don't just happen randomly or because of a good luck or a bad luck factor. We are not merely a physical entity. Man is a living soul. In a very practical way, there should be an understanding about God and what He has done and is doing in a universe He has created. Every person has the capacity to understand and know that God exists. The mind of mankind has become corrupted by various influences such as evolutionary thought, atheistic influence, secular humanism and progressivism. There is a mindset among a growing number of people who block all things eternal from the existent culture and any acknowledgement by the inhabitants of the planet earth. However, there are certain truths that are undeniable. Ecclesiastes

3:10-14 (NKJV) contains a fascinating concept. "I have seen the God-given task with which the sons of men are to be occupied. He has made everything beautiful in its time. Also He has put eternity in their hearts, except that no one can find out the work that God does from beginning to end. I know that nothing is better for them than to rejoice, and to do good in their lives, and also that every man should eat and drink and enjoy the good of all his labor--it is the gift of God." In particular, the phrase that stands out is, "He has put eternity in their hearts." The soul and spirit of man has been created with eternity in His heart. Until one comes to God through Jesus Christ, that inner sense of eternity will be a desire that needs to be met and satisfied. One can deny it, ignore it, attempt to suppress it, but it is there and longs for something to fill that void and vacuum. Eternity in his heart means that a part of man will never die. Along with eternity in his heart there will also be the sense that there is a purpose in and for life. One may not always comprehend the detail and meaning of that purpose but there is that sense deep within the heart of mankind. This sense will become more apparent as the acknowledgement of Him becomes a solid belief that God exists. The One who created man is the One who desires fellowship and communion with His creation. This is apparent in Jeremiah 29:11-14 (NIV) by means of the Lord's message to His people who have been in captivity for a long time. The Babylonians had carried off the people of God and subjected them to various inconveniences and their national practices. The Lord declares, "For I know the plans I have for you, plans to prosper you and not to harm you, plans to give you hope and a future. Then you will call upon me and come and pray to me, and I will listen to you. You will seek me and find me when you seek me with all your heart. I will be found by you and will bring you back from captivity. I will gather you from all the nations and places where I have banished you and will bring you back to the place from which I carried you into exile." God does not forget His own.

He knows where everyone is and why they are where they are. There are hard and difficult times that one may pass through but oftentimes these become occasions when God gains the attention of those who had been indifferent toward Him or disobedient to Him.

Even if a person never hears a spoken word about God, there are at least two factors one needs to weigh. The first is in Psalm 19:1 (NKJV), "The heavens declare the glory of God; and the firmament shows His handiwork." The Creation and the Universe demonstrate the handiwork of an all-powerful and unlimited God. The fact of the entire universe being in an orbit that is precise and exact should cause one to acknowledge that it was designed and made by God. The second is Romans 2:14-15 (NKJV), "For when Gentiles, who do not have the law, by nature do the things in the law, these, although not having the law, are a law to themselves, who show the work of the law written in their hearts, their conscience also bearing witness, and between themselves their thoughts accusing or else excusing them." *The Message Paraphrase* states it as plainly as possible, "When outsiders who have never heard of God's law follow it more or less by instinct, they confirm its truth by their obedience. They show that God's law is not something alien, imposed on us from without, but woven into the very fabric of our creation. There is something deep within them that echoes God's yes and no, right and wrong."

When *The Message Paraphrase* makes the statement, "There is something deep within them that echoes God's yes and no, right and wrong," it is allowing that conscience and awareness is present within all and the sense of right and wrong is present in all. The field of psychology is concerned with the study of the nature of conscience and its relation to man's other moral capabilities. Psychology tries to ascertain two things: Is conscience a natural human trait innate to man, or is it the result of upbringing and conditioned by those circumstances of life which affect man's formation? Is conscience a manifestation of the mind, the senses or the will of man, or is it a manifestation of some independent power? The overall consideration is that God puts the sense of the moral law within mankind. Man can attempt to suppress it or perform in such a lawless manner that his conscience becomes seared and desensitized to any right or wrong considerations. The idea of the seared conscience is stated in I Timothy 4:1-3 (ESV), "Now the Spirit expressly says that in later times some will depart from the faith by devoting themselves to deceitful spirits and teachings of demons, through the insincerity of liars whose consciences are seared, who forbid marriage and require abstinence from foods that God created to be received with thanksgiving by those who believe and know the truth." When one observes that the culture is being corrupted and the moral values are being jettisoned, it is a clear indication that one may be living in the "later times" mentioned in this passage.

Charles Finney was an evangelist in the 19th Century. In a lecture given on April 28, 1841, he taught and discussed, "How The Conscience Becomes Seared." He presented this lecture with 31 sub-heads. Among them are: "(1) The conscience becomes seared by the will resisting the affirmations of reason. The conscience is now generally supposed to be a function of the reason. Whether it is regarded in this light or not, it is certain that it becomes seared when the will opposes itself and continues opposed to the decisions of the reason. (2) Especially does the conscience become seared, when the will persists in courses directly denounced or condemned by the conscience. In such cases the conscience soon becomes indignantly silent and leaves the soul stupefied to pursue its course of disobedience. (3) It is often seared by an individual's resorting to sophistry (a plausible but misleading or fallacious argument) to justify any course of disobedience. (7) Indulgence in known sin of any kind will greatly and rapidly sear your conscience. (8) Especially indulgence in presumptuous sins or those sins already put under the condemning sentence of conscience. Whenever conscience has called your attention to the sinfulness of any act or course of action and you still persist in it, this is a presumptuous sin, and such a course will soon cause your conscience to become seared with a hot iron."

How serious is the presumptuous sin? What level of concern should one have in this regard? One can learn a valuable lesson by the words of David in Psalm 19:7-13 (ESV), "The law of the Lord is perfect, reviving the soul; the testimony of the Lord is sure, making wise the simple; the precepts of the Lord are right, rejoicing the heart; the commandment of the Lord is pure, enlightening the eyes; the fear of the Lord is clean, enduring forever; the rules of the Lord are true, and righteous altogether. More to be desired are they than gold, even much fine gold; sweeter also than honey and drippings of the honeycomb. Moreover, by them is your servant warned; in keeping them there is great reward. Who can discern his errors? Declare me innocent from hidden faults. Keep back your servant also from presumptuous sins; let them not have dominion over me! Then I shall be blameless, and innocent of great transgression." A passage such as this would serve one well as a testimony and a prayer. All of us have the capability and propensity to sin in thought, word and deed. The one who has retained a sensitive conscience will be more aware of these areas of sin and sinning. It does not occur because one sets out to live on the margins of life by keeping one foot in the secular world and the other in the spiritual world. It is because of a sinful nature that is in the process of being renewed and restored. It is the process where one is being sanctified wherein one is enabled to die more and more to sin. Conversely one will live more and more unto righteousness. We are under construction and God isn't done with us yet. We are being shaped to be more and more conformed to the image of Christ. The *Westminster Shorter Catechism* (Q. 35) states, "Sanctification is the work of God's free grace, whereby we are renewed in the whole man, after the image of God, and are enabled more and more to die unto sin, and live unto righteousness." It is "the work of God's free grace" and it is being accomplished in God's people.

Another aspect of "in all your ways acknowledge Him" is that one has to believe there is a God. When one begins to read the Holy Scriptures, the first statement that appears is Genesis 1:1 (NKJV), "In the beginning, God created..." In Hebrews 1:1-3 (NIV) we read how God has spoken, "In the past God spoke to our forefathers through the prophets at many times and in various ways, but in these last days he has spoken to us by his Son, whom he appointed heir of all things, and through whom he made the universe. The Son is the radiance of God's glory and the exact representation of his being, sustaining all things by his powerful word. After he had provided purification for sins, he sat down at the right hand of the Majesty in heaven." The manner by which He has spoken to us by His Son is further amplified in John 1:1-4 (NIV), "In the beginning was the Word, and the Word was with God, and the Word was God. He was with God in the beginning. Through him all things were made; without him nothing was made that has been made. In him was life, and that life was the light of men." To embrace these truths so that one can implement "in all your ways acknowledge Him" is given in Hebrews 11:1, 6 (NIV), "Now faith is being sure of what we hope for and certain of what we do not see. And without faith it is impossible to please God, because anyone who comes to him must believe that he exists and that he rewards those who earnestly seek him."

"In all our ways acknowledge Him" will occur only as one has exercised faith by believing that God exists. For the "little boats, little people and other sheep" this is where the playing field becomes level. The "all" and "whosoever" in Scripture includes everyone. Before God, everyone is significant and everyone has worth. There is no class distinction or ethnic discrimination in the heart and mind of God. The only issue is whether or not one believes in God and God alone. In many churches, a Creedal Statement, *The Apostles' Creed*, is used as part of their ritual or order of service. Congregations are asked a question: "Christian! What is it that you believe?" A variant sometimes used: "Brothers and Sisters in Christ, What is it that you believe?" It other places it is prefaced by: "Let us give affirmation to our faith." Whatever the form or ritual, the congregant is expected to respond: "I believe in God the Father Almighty, Maker of heaven and earth, and in Jesus Christ, His only Son, our Lord, Who was conceived by the Holy Spirit..." If you had to give an explanation for what you have stated from The Apostles' Creed, what is it that you have declared and affirmed? Are you able to prove from the Holy Scriptures that which you have declared you believe? Why must you be prepared and ready to give an answer for what you believe? When Jude (NIV) wrote his epistle, part of the burden of his heart was expressed in verses 3 and 4, "Beloved, although I was very eager to write to you about our common salvation, I found it necessary to write appealing to you to contend for the faith that was once for all delivered to the saints. For certain people have crept in unnoticed who long ago were designated for this condemnation, ungodly people, who pervert the grace of our God into sensuality and deny our only Master and Lord, Jesus Christ." Note the urgency in what he wrote, "I found it necessary to write appealing to you to contend for the faith". Why this urgency? There is urgency because there are "ungodly people, who pervert the grace of our God into sensuality and deny our only Master and Lord, Jesus Christ." Each of us need to study the Scriptures, and know them, and to be able to "contend for the faith" in order to be useful in making the foundations of what we believe viable and understandable by all. Even if there are those who reject the message of what we believe, they will be left without excuse before the Almighty God.

    Not only must one know what he or she believes, it is vital that one's life is lived in accordance with that belief system. It

12. A Serious Acknowledgement

includes and entails how one responds to the Lordship of Jesus Christ in one's life. This goal and standard is basic to one's submission to Christ in everything. Paul established a standard for submission to Christ when he wrote in II Corinthians 10:4-5 (NIV), "The weapons we fight with are not the weapons of the world. On the contrary, they have divine power to demolish strongholds. We demolish arguments and every pretension that sets itself up against the knowledge of God, and we take captive every thought to make it obedient to Christ." There are two prongs to Paul's thrust: to "demolish arguments and every pretension that sets itself up against the knowledge of God" and to "take captive every thought to make it obedient to Christ."

In this regard, it is important for one to have a clear understanding of the truth about God. In a broad view, it would be in the category of Christian apologetics. Under the heading of, Christian scholarship and the defense of the faith - The Importance of Christian scholarship in the defense of the faith, J. Gresham Machen gave an address in London on June 17, 1932. He said, "The Apostle Paul in the First Epistle to the Thessalonians gives a precious summary of his missionary preaching. He does so by telling what it was to which the Thessalonians turned when they were saved. Was it a mere program of life to which they turned? Was it a simple faith, in the modern sense which divorces faith from knowledge and supposes that a man can have simple faith in a person of whom he knows nothing or about whom he holds opinions that make faith in him absurd? Not at all. In turning to Christ, the Thessalonians turned to a whole system of theology. "Ye turned to God from idols, to serve the living and true God; and to wait for His Son from heaven, whom He raised from the dead, even Jesus, who delivers us from the wrath to come." "Ye turned to God from idols" - There is theology proper. "And to wait for His Son from heaven" - There is Christology. "Whom He raised from the dead" - There is the supernatural act of God in history. "Even

Jesus" - There is the humanity of our Lord. "Who delivers us from the wrath to come?" - There is the Christian doctrine of sin and the Christian doctrine of the Cross of Christ." Dr. Machen continued, "The New Testament gives not one bit of comfort to those who separate faith from knowledge, to those who hold the absurd view that a man can trust a person about whom he knows nothing. What many men despise today as doctrine, the New Testament calls the Gospel; and the New Testament treats it as the message upon which salvation depends. But if that be so, if salvation depends upon the message in which Christ is offered as Savior, it is obviously important that we should get the message straight. That is where Christian scholarship comes in. Christian scholarship is important in order that we may tell the story of Jesus and His love straight and full and plain."

  If one is to implement "in all your ways acknowledge Him" in one's life, it requires that one become fully acquainted with God and Jesus Christ. This is the idea and thrust of Paul in Philippians 3:8-12 (NIV), "What is more, I consider everything a loss compared to the surpassing greatness of knowing Christ Jesus my Lord, for whose sake I have lost all things. I consider them rubbish, that I may gain Christ and be found in him, not having a righteousness of my own that comes from the law, but that which is through faith in Christ, the righteousness that comes from God and is by faith. I want to know Christ and the power of his resurrection and the fellowship of sharing in his sufferings, becoming like him in his death, and so, somehow, to attain to the resurrection from the dead. Not that I have already obtained all this, or have already been made perfect, but I press on to take hold of that for which Christ Jesus took hold of me." There is an intensity and urgency that compels Paul to remain focused on the goal and to keep pursuing the prize. The emphasis of Paul is clear in terms of the goal he will pursue: I want to know "the surpassing greatness of knowing Christ Jesus my Lord;" and "I want to know Christ;" I also want to know "the power of his resurrection;" and "I want to know the fellowship of sharing in his sufferings;" I want to know the fullness of what it is to "become like him in his death, and so, somehow, to attain to the resurrection from the dead." He wants to know the completeness and the reality of oneness in Christ, and intimacy to the highest level and greatest degree. He had come to the place in his life where "in all your ways acknowledge Him" was not just a phrase to affirm but a lifestyle to attain. It was not theoretical but a practical reality. He realized that he needed to know Him in order that he could clearly and forthrightly make Him known.

The example of The Berean believers should be a continuing challenge for the Church and Christian community in current times. In Acts 17:10-12 (NIV) we read, "Now the Bereans were of more noble character than the Thessalonians, for they received the message with great eagerness and examined the Scriptures every day to see if what Paul said was true. Many of the Jews believed, as did also a number of prominent Greek women and many Greek men." What made the Berean believers so unique? It was their basic devotion to learn about God and in all their ways to acknowledge Him. There was a first step that they followed, namely, "They received the message with great eagerness and examined the Scriptures every day to see if what Paul said was true." It was a form of biblical Hermeneutics where the text and words were studied. There would be a comparison with other Scriptures so they could arrive at a determination that what Paul was teaching was consistent with and confirmed by other Scriptures. In their "great eagerness" to know, they wanted to determine the accuracy of what they had heard. Just as they demonstrated an eagerness to hear and know, they also possessed an eagerness to share and teach others. They were noble and devout and committed to knowing Him. This commitment would better equip them to reach all kinds of people including "the little boats, the little people and the other sheep."

They would demonstrate that no one was unimportant, expendable, unnecessary, inconsequential or insignificant.

APPLICATIONS and QUESTIONS:

What is the best way for you to implement on a regular basis "in all your ways acknowledge Him"? Is this just for children and young people?

Do you tend to act toward the "little boats, little people and other sheep" as though they were insignificant, expendable, worthless?

Do you think about "when bad things happen to good people" and do you wonder why that is thought to be the case? Explain!

What if the question was reversed to read, "when good things happen to bad people?" How do you explain it?

Have you ever heard of "common grace"? How does "common grace" apply to the wicked and the righteous? Give at least two illustrations in your answer.

Aside from Church related Bible Studies and Groups, do you personally do an intensive and deductive Bible Study? How often? Daily? Occasionally?

If you were called upon to give a reason for the hope that is in you, what would you say and where would you begin? Why?

Why do you use the Bible as your source and resource Book?
What would you say to a person about his or her need to Know God and to put his or her faith and trust in God alone? Where would you begin?

What is the importance of biblical apologetics and hermeneutics? Can you define these terms? Why is it important to know what you believe and why you believe it?

Have you ever met a person who impressed you that they had a "seared conscience"? What made you reach that determination? Does that mean a person has crossed a line and is beyond any hope or the grace of God?

What are two major causes that result in a "seared conscience"?

In Ephesians 4:30-32, there is a list of things that are stated to "grieve the Holy Spirit". If someone does "grieve the Holy Spirit" does that represent a "seared conscience" or something else?

Do you know individuals within the Church who are given to "bitterness, wrath, anger, malice, and evil-speaking"? Do they have a seared conscience? Is such a one a Christian? In your opinion, will he or she be numbered with the sheep or goats?

How well do you think you know the Triune God?

How well do you think you are able to make the Triune God known?

What is your sense of the times in which we live? Are we approaching the time when "the church" will be persecuted?

In conjunction with your answer to the above question, read the following from I Peter 4:17-19 (NKJV), "For the time has come for judgment to begin at the house of God; and if it begins with us first, what will be the end of those who do not obey the gospel of God? Now, if the righteous one is scarcely saved, where will the ungodly and the sinner appear? Therefore let those who suffer according to the will of God commit their souls to Him in doing good, as to a faithful Creator." Does your answer regarding the persecuted Church coincide with this passage?

Do you really know my Jesus? Do your really know my Lord?
Do you really know my Jesus? Are you trusting in His Word?

Yes, I really know your Jesus! Yes, I really know your Lord!
Now, I really know my Jesus! I am trusting in His word!
An Old Camp Chorus - Author Unknown

13. A Serious Performance

In a recent book I wrote, *Taking A Serious God Seriously*, I attached a summary paragraph that indicated Daniel has been summoned before the king to interpret the writing on the wall of the palace after a hand had suddenly appeared and a finger wrote Mene, Mene, Tekel, Parsin. Daniel was able to interpret the writing was a warning to the king that his Kingdom is going to end (you have been weighed in the balance of God and been found wanting). The king had failed to understand his need to *Take A Serious God Seriously*. Because of that, the judgment of God would come upon him and the nation (the nation divided between the Medes and the Persians). God is very serious about sin and the ways in which it becomes so easily condoned by those who are identified as His people. The day is coming when all of one's professions, deeds and actions will be weighed in God's eternal scale. When you are weighed in God's balances, will you be found wanting? With that summary in mind and the changes in governments that have so quickly accelerated in the Middle East and Europe in recent times, the thoughtful person needs to consider these realities and the brevity of life, along with a renewed emphasis and focus upon this thought, serious times require people who are serious. In *Matthew Henry's Concise Commentary* on I Peter 4:12-17, he states, "A time of universal calamity was at hand, as foretold by our Savior, Matthew 24:9-10. And if such things befall in this life, how awful will the day of judgment be! It is true that the righteous are scarcely saved; even those who endeavor to walk uprightly in the ways of God. This does not mean that the purpose and performance of God are uncertain, but only the great difficulties and hard encounters in the way; that they go through so many temptations and tribulations, so many fightings without and fears within." There is an important phrase used, namely, "the purpose and performance of God."

In the "Faith and Reason" section of *USA Today* for August 11, 2011, the column was headlined, "Stephen Colbert Questions God's Job Performance." The columnist identified himself as a sincere Catholic and a satirist. He goes on to state, "We're mad at Congress, mad at President Obama, mad at Wall Street. Can't anyone live up to their job description? What about God? How's His performance these days? The column continued, "And for answers, he turned to the official Chaplain of the Colbert Nation, Rev. James Martin, culture editor for *America Magazine* and author of *The Jesuit Guide to (Almost) Everything*. There is an interesting comment made in the column, "For answers on why can't we judge God, or why His approval ratings are so low or why bad things happen, Martin has his usual witty, while-faithful answers. God's mystery is still beyond us but while we ponder it, Martin says, maybe we should come up with some gratitude, not complain all the time." The statement of interest and one that should be noticed is, "Maybe we should come up with some gratitude, not complain all the time."

The broad question of Colbert is thought provoking. He asked, "What about God? How's His performance these days?" In a previous chapter, there is a similar discussion. What about God? Is He being acknowledged in all of our ways? Let us focus briefly on the second question of Colbert, "What About The Performance of God?" What is it that God does? One answer to this broad question is that God always acts in accordance with His character, purpose, nature, will and attributes. We know that He cannot and does not lie (Hebrews 6:18 and Titus 1:2, NIV). We know that God cannot deny Himself (II Timothy 2:11-13, NKJV). We know that He is unlimited in terms of what He can and will do (Psalm 147:5 and Ephesians 3:20, NIV). Ephesians 1:3-11 (ESV), gives a response in terms of the "Performance of God." It is not an exhaustive list but a starting place of what God has done "according to the purpose of His will." The text states some of the things God does (numbers added for emphasis):

> (1) He has blessed us in Christ with every spiritual blessing in the heavenly places;
>
> (2) He chose us in him before the foundation of the world, that we should be holy and blameless before him;
>
> (3) In love, He predestined us;
>
> (4) He adopted us as sons through Jesus Christ, according to the purpose of his will, to the praise of his glorious grace, with which he has blessed us in the Beloved;
>
> (5) In Jesus Christ, He has redemption through his blood;
>
> (6) He has provided forgiveness for our trespasses;
>
> (7) He made this provision according to the riches of his grace, which He lavished upon us;
>
> (8) He has made known to us (in all wisdom and insight) the mystery of his will, according to his purpose, which He set forth in Christ as a plan for the fullness of time, to unite all things in him, things in heaven and things on earth.
>
> (9) In Jesus Christ, He has granted us as inheritance, inasmuch as we have been predestined according to the purpose of him who works all things according to the counsel of his will.

The problem in understanding the ways, purposes, and performance of God is the result of an ignorance of the Word of God, and the influential false preachers and teachers in any given time-frame. In Jeremiah's day, false preaching and teaching was rampant. God's people were about to be taken off into captivity. Even though a message of warning from God was issued, it was not heeded and that which was false became the religion of a people who would soon perish. There is a brief description of an awful and dreadful day given in Jeremiah 23:9-13 (ESV), "Concerning the prophets: My heart is broken within me; all my bones shake; I am like a drunken man, like a man overcome by wine, because of the Lord and because of his holy words. For the land is full of adulterers; because of the curse the land mourns, and the pastures of the wilderness are dried up. Their course is evil, and their might is not right. Both prophet and priest are ungodly; even in my house I have found their evil, declares the Lord. Therefore their way shall be to them like slippery paths in the darkness, into which they shall be driven and fall, for I will bring disaster upon them in the year of their punishment, declares the Lord. In the prophets of Samaria I saw an unsavory thing: they prophesied by Baal and led my people Israel astray." In verses 9 and 10 (NLT), the text states, "For the prophets do evil and abuse their power. The priests are like the prophets, all ungodly, wicked men. I have seen their despicable acts right here in my own Temple, says the Lord." If the prophets are wicked and unfaithful in the task of communicating the Word of the Lord, and if the priests are ungodly and practice that which is despicable, how can the people know the truth that God wants proclaimed? If their sense of hearing has been dulled, and their consciences seared, how will the people be able to respond? The prophets and priests have done extensive damage. Their wicked behavior and blasphemous ways have perverted not only the message from the Lord, but the entire culture of their day. What about the "little boats, little people and the other sheep" who have been treated as though they were insignificant, of little or no consequence, and as those without much worth? Who will rescue them from the cultural quagmire? Who will demonstrate care and compassion toward them?

The evil work by evil men has many subtleties that tend to delude and beguile multitudes of people. In all generations when this occurs, the spiritual erosion begins in subtle ways and escalates to a full-blown rejection of God and the embrace of demonic illusions. What are some of the subtleties that have resulted in such a condition? When and how did it begin? One of the contributing factors is the cultural revolution that has taken place in our nation and world. The cultural revolution can be summarized as being a quest of sorts: Culture is an attempt to find a coherent set of answers to the existential questions we all have about life. Therefore a genuine cultural revolution is one that makes a decisive break from the shared meanings of the past, especially relating to the meaning (and origin) of life. Solomon raised a question in this regard when he wrote in Ecclesiastes 3:9-11 (NLT), "What do people really get for all their hard work? I have thought about this in connection with the various kinds of work God has given people to do. God has made everything beautiful for its own time. He has planted eternity in the human heart, but even so, people cannot see the whole scope of God's work from beginning to end." The MSG Paraphrase renders these words with a sound of bewilderment, frustration and mystery: "But in the end, does it really make a difference what anyone does? I've had a good look at what God has given us to do - busywork, mostly. True, God made everything beautiful in itself and in its time - but he's left us in the dark, so we can never know what God is up to, whether he's coming or going." The question before us: Has God left us in the dark? Has God failed to indicate to us what He is up to? Has God been silent in terms of His coming and going, His eternal plan and purpose for us and the world? We need to pause and realize that serious times require people who are serious, to take a serious God seriously and to believe the Word of God that tells us what man is to believe concerning God and what duty God requires of His creatures.

The subtlety of false teaching and degraded standards is the impact it has among those who have been corrupted by it. We need to contrast Solomon's thought regarding, "eternity in the heart of man," with the thought of Jeremiah 17:9-10 (NKJV), "The heart is deceitful above all things, And desperately wicked; Who can know it? I, the Lord, search the heart, I test the mind, Even to give every man according to his ways, According to the fruit of his doings." Jesus Christ gives a cautionary word regarding the potential of the heart of man: "But those things which proceed out of the mouth come from the heart, and they defile a man. For out of the heart proceed evil thoughts, murders, adulteries, fornications, thefts, false witness, blasphemies. These are the things which defile a man" (Matthew 15:18-19, NKJV). The overall point is that the Word of God establishes an expectation. A person is to embrace and his life is to be lived with a sense of eternity and a commitment to guard oneself appropriately so that it does not become susceptible to false teaching, as well as the carnal and wicked temptations that can infiltrate one's life. The word of wisdom in Proverbs 4:23 (NKJV) should be incorporated into one's practice of pure religion, namely, "Keep your heart with all diligence, for out of it spring the issues of life." The New Living Translation is helpful when it renders this verse, "Above all else, guard your heart, for it affects everything you do."

As one considers the "Performance of God," His long-suffering nature serves to bring His people to Himself. We note Exodus 34:4-7 (ESV), "So Moses cut two tablets of stone like the first. And he rose early in the morning and went up on Mount Sinai, as the Lord had commanded him, and took in his hand two tablets of stone. The Lord descended in the cloud and stood with him there, and proclaimed the name of the Lord. The Lord passed before him and proclaimed, The Lord, the Lord, a God merciful and gracious, slow to anger, and abounding in steadfast love and faithfulness, keeping steadfast love for thousands, forgiving iniquity and transgression and sin, but who will by no means clear the guilty, visiting the iniquity of the fathers on the children and the children's children, to the third and the fourth generation." In verses 6-7 (NKJV), the translation is, "And the Lord passed before him and proclaimed, The Lord, the Lord God, merciful and gracious, long-suffering, and abounding in goodness and truth, keeping mercy for thousands, forgiving iniquity and transgression and sin." One should never forget that God is merciful, gracious, long-suffering, abounding in goodness and truth, and forgiving.

In terms of the "Performance of God," in a passage that speaks of the coming judgment of God and the destruction of all things, Peter wrote: "Beloved, do not forget this one thing, that with the Lord one day is as a thousand years, and a thousand years as one day. The Lord is not slack concerning His promise, as some count slackness, but is long-suffering toward us, not willing that any should perish but that all should come to repentance. But the day of the Lord will come as a thief in the night, in which the heavens will pass away with a great noise, and the elements will melt with fervent heat; both the earth and the works that are in it will be burned up. Therefore, since all these things will be dissolved, what manner of persons ought you to be in holy conduct and godliness, looking for and hastening the coming of the day of God" (II Peter 3:8-11, NIV). It is clear that The Lord is long-suffering and patient. The Lord wants people to come to repentance, seek His face and walk in His ways. Those who do not respond to His desire for them to repent can be certain that judgment, a very fierce and complete judgment, will occur and "...the elements will melt with fervent heat; both the earth and the works that are in it will be burned up." How that judgment will occur, we don't know. When that judgment will occur, has not been revealed. The how and when are both an integral part of the "Performance of God." It will certainly take place. One would be wise to respond to the love, mercy and grace of God. There is a terminating point with the Lord being long-suffering and patient. The time for repentance is now. As the Word of God states, (II Corinthians 6:2, NKJV), "In an acceptable time I have heard you, and in the day of salvation I have helped you. Behold, now is the accepted time; behold, now is the day of salvation." This is God's message of hope for all. It also includes those who are so often and easily neglected or forgotten - "the little boats, the little people and the other sheep."

APPLICATIONS and QUESTIONS:

How serious do you think God is regarding judgment upon this world?

How seriously do you believe people are in hearing and heeding God's Word?

Within "the Church, do the "people of God" take the Word of God as seriously as they should? Why do you think that is?

In terms of the "purpose and performance of God," how well do you think you understand it? What would you like to know or have answered?

If a serious God is serious about what He has spoken through His Word, what should the degree of urgency be with the people in the churches?

In what ways do people misconstrue God being long-suffering? What is their rationale for doing so?

There is a group of questions in this chapter that should receive response:

Has God left us in the dark?
Has God failed to indicate to us what He is up to?
Has God been silent in terms of His coming and going, His eternal plan and purpose for us and the world?

> *Though millions have found him a friend,*
> *And have turned from the sins they have sinned;*
> *The Savior still waits to open the gates*
> *And welcome a sinner before it's too late.*
>
> *Refrain:*
> *There's room at the cross for you.*
> *There's room at the cross for you.*
> *Though millions have come, there's still room for one,*
> *Yes, there's room at the cross for you.*

Ira F. Stanphill

Concluding Thoughts

The metaphor that has been used in these chapters is based upon the words in Mark 4:36 (NIV), "Leaving the crowd behind, they took him along, just as he was, in the boat. There were also other boats with him." The metaphor was employed to include and represent "little people" and "other sheep." The idea was to communicate that there is no one who is unimportant, or inconsequential, or insignificant, or unworthy in God's sight. The "little boat, little people and other sheep" should never be disregarded or deemed to be either incapable or insignificant. The words of Isaiah 40:10-11, ESV are an encouragement to all who are the "little boats, little people and other sheep." The text indicates, "Behold, the Lord God comes with might, and His arm rules for Him; behold, His reward is with Him, and His recompense before Him. He will tend His flock like a shepherd; He will gather the lambs in His arms; He will carry them in His bosom, and gently lead those that are with young." In the NLT, the verses are paraphrased to indicate; "the Sovereign Lord is coming in all his glorious power. He will rule with awesome strength. See, He brings His reward with Him as He comes. He will feed His flock like a shepherd. He will carry the lambs in His arms, holding them close to His heart. He will gently lead the mother sheep with their young." All of those who are seen as the "little boats, little people and other sheep" should be encouraged and filled with expectation by these words

In this regard, an illustration that should touch one's heart appeared in *Our Daily Bread* on December 07, 2014, written by Dave Branon. It was entitled, Johnny's Race. He might've been easily relegated to the status of being unimportant, inconsequential, unworthy or insignificant in terms of ability or doing any competitive physical activity. The devotional indicates the following about

Johnny: "When 19-year-old Johnny Agar finished the 5k race, he had a lot of people behind him—family members and friends who were celebrating his accomplishment. Johnny has cerebral palsy, which makes physical activity difficult. But he and his dad, Jeff, have teamed up to compete in many races—Dad pushing and Johnny riding. But one day, Johnny wanted to finish by himself. Halfway through the race, his dad took him out of his cart, helped him to his walker, and assisted Johnny as he completed the race on his own two feet. That led to a major celebration as friends and family cheered his accomplishment. 'It made it easier for me to do it with them behind me,' Johnny told a reporter. 'The encouragement is what drove me.' Isn't that what Christ-followers are meant to do? Hebrews 10:24 reminds us: Let us consider how we may spur one another on toward love and good deeds (NIV)."

No one should under-estimate the value of another regarding what they can or cannot do. If the principle of encouragement was more prominent and a rule for one's life, it could be used in a positive way to focus one's attention on a meaningful course for his life. It is similar to creating a thirst and hunger to strive for that which is better and will result in a positive contribution being made within a misdirected culture. Part of the reason for this emphasis of this book is a person with whom I have been acquainted for several years. He would easily be the personification of a "little boat" just bobbing along on the surface or drifting without a sure destination. He was born into a poor family and lived in a neighborhood and housing that left much to be desired. Even though he would go to Church, he was mostly just there and never felt accepted in any group. He was a classic "little boat" that could easily fall through the cracks of life. If that was his plight, few would have thought anything about it. No one would've missed him or inquired about him. There were some people, all too few, who reached out to him and accepted him as he was, but interestingly, some of those who reached out were "other little boats" themselves.

He attended public schools but his high school years were very difficult. He was very much alone and with very few people who could be called friends. Despite that rather directionless and meaningless background, he drifted to a college that accepted him as a student. His life began to change when he met a young woman who not only became a friend, but one who would also love him. They were married and he continued his studies in college. After graduation, he attended a seminary and began to prepare for Church ministry. After he graduated from seminary and headed out with his family to begin his labor as a pastor, he did so with enthusiasm, vision and ideals. Over the years, his enthusiasm and vision never changed but his ideals were very quickly dashed. He remembered an older Pastor sharing with him that his ideals were correct and that he should never lose them. However, the older pastor went on to tell him that it would be best to put his ideals in his back pocket and remember what and where they are. He wanted to convey that few Churches are eager to embrace ideals that require change. Regrettably, the older Pastor was correct in his evaluation of the Church and the refusal of many to be led.

His disappointment as a young pastor was similar to that of the years of his youth where he felt alone, unaccepted and treated as though he was of little consequence, worth or significance. His sense was that some Churches can be very harsh, especially as they allow the culture of the world to govern their behavior in the Church. While his heart's desire had been to serve a church for an extended period of time, maybe for his entire life, that was not to be the case. He moved several times with his family to different places where his desire to serve as a pastor never waned. Although he could have easily become discouraged or disengaged, he never did. He and his bride were among those who made a commitment to go anywhere, at any time, to do any work, at any cost for the Lord. The journey was not always easy for him and disappointments were several. He remembered how he and his wife embraced each other and claimed once again Psalm 37:23-26 (NIV), "If the Lord delights in a man's way, he makes his steps firm; though he stumble, he will not fall, for the Lord upholds him with his hand. I was young and now I am old, yet I have never seen the righteous forsaken or their children begging bread. They are always generous and lend freely; their children will be blessed." With those words of affirmation and encouragement, he pressed on toward completion of the task the Lord gave him to do. Amid the disappointments, his motivation was to implement as best he could the words in Acts 20:24 (NIV), "If only I may finish the race and complete the task the Lord Jesus has given me, the task of testifying to the gospel of God's grace."

Perhaps, you have felt like you were being viewed as a "little boat" or categorized as one relegated to the grouping of those considered to be the "little people or other sheep." You may have felt that you were seen or treated as being unworthy, unnecessary, inconsequential or insignificant. It is important to remember that you are precious in the sight of the Lord. If you had been the only little boat, or little person, or other sheep on this planet, you would have been important enough to become the one who "God so loved, that He gave His only begotten Son, that if you believed in Him, you should not perish but have everlasting life" (Personal Paraphrase of John 3:16). It would also be helpful to remember that you are who you are for God's purpose. Jeremiah 29:11 (NIV) should also be in one's heart and mind, "For I know the plans I have for you, declares the Lord, plans to prosper you and not to harm you, plans to give you hope and a future." Take note of these words: "He has plans to PROSPER YOU, plans to GIVE YOU HOPE and a FUTURE." Be encouraged by the Word of the Lord and keep on looking to Jesus, the author and finisher of your faith. As you continue on your journey, try to remember some of the song written by Bill and Gloria Gaither.

I am a promise. I am a possibility.

I am a promise with a capital "P".
I am a great big bundle of potentiality.
I'm a promise to be anything God wants me to be.

As a footnote to the above Concluding Thoughts, I can remember most of the detail of that life, because that person was this author, just another "little boat" and identified among the "little people" but redeemed from among the "other sheep" and brought into the fold of The Good Shepherd. In retrospect and to some degree, I am able to say in the words of I Corinthians 15:10 (NIV), "But by the grace of God I am what I am, and his grace to me was not without effect. No, I worked harder than all of them, yet not I, but the grace of God that was with me." I, and my companion on this journey, my Peggy, can gratefully acknowledge, "To God Be The Glory, Great Things He Has Done" and is doing.

Thank you for reading this book and for doing the attached studies. May your life be blest and enriched by our God and Savior.

Be Thou my Vision, O Lord of my heart;
Naught be all else to me, save that Thou art.
Thou my best Thought, by day or by night,
Waking or sleeping, Thy presence my light.

Riches I heed not, nor man's empty praise,
Thou mine Inheritance, now and always:
Thou and Thou only, first in my heart,
High King of Heaven, my Treasure Thou art.

High King of Heaven, my victory won,
May I reach Heaven's joys, O bright Heaven's Sun!
Heart of my own heart, whatever befall,
Still be my Vision, O Ruler of all.

Dallan Forgaill, 8th Century

Concluding Thoughts

About the Author

    I, the third of three children, was born in Brooklyn, New York and lived the first 20 years of my life there. After High School, I had given no consideration for any further schooling. Any thought of a Bible College and preparing for ministry was far removed from my thinking. I was content with driving a delivery truck for an auto supply dealer. However, the Lord had different plans for my life to get me from where I was to where He wanted me to be. I had an accident with the truck and the owner was upset about it. I decided that I no longer wanted to work for him and left his employ abruptly.

    It was at this time that the Founder of Lakeside Bible Conference spoke at the church I was attending. Following the service, I volunteered to be a worker at Lakeside Bible Conference in Carmel, New York. During the summer of 1954, I met several people who were already in a Bible College or preparing to enter their Freshman year. I stayed in a two-man cabin with a man who was President of the Student Body at Columbia Bible College (now Columbia International University) in Columbia, South Carolina. We had been assigned to work with teenagers from New York City. However, during the course of the summer, he would frequently ask me whether or not I had ever thought about what God's will and plan for my life might be. His question "bugged" me and I did my best to avoid him and the question. However, it was the beginning point of my pilgrimage in ministry.

    His persistence planted a seed that became watered by Columbia Bible College. At the end of the summer, some friends who had pre-enrolled at Columbia Bible College invited me to ride to South Carolina with them and then to hitch-hike back home. I had no other plans and decided to go with them. I was invited to enroll for the Freshmen Class by some staff members of the college.

I did so and that led to my also going on to attend Covenant Theological Seminary in St. Louis, MO and to begin an active ministry that is now in its fifty-first year. I had not given much thought to publishing a book but a young man from a former Pastorate is now the owner of Theocentric Publishing Group. It was with his encouragement that I have written some books and had them published by Theocentric Publishing Group. Two of the more recent books published are: *Taking A Serious God Seriously*, and *Amid The Cultural Chaos*. There are now two sequel books on the cultural chaos, *Trending Toward Cultural Captivity* and the newest volume is *Navigating The Cultural Maze*. These and other titles are available through Theocentric Publishing Group or Amazon (http://www.amazon.com/-/e/B004S1X6J4).

www.ingramcontent.com/pod-product-compliance
Lightning Source LLC
Chambersburg PA
CBHW061645040426
42446CB00010B/1583